Life Reset

A Guide for Women to Recenter & Overcome Burnout

Life Reset

A Guide for Women to Recenter & Overcome Burnout

Lisa Macedo, LMFT

The scenarios presented in this workbook are inspired by true events and the author's professional and personal experiences. To protect privacy, details have been changed and fictionalized characters are used. These examples are intended for illustrative purposes only.

This book is intended for educational and informational purposes only. It is not intended to be, nor should it be considered, a substitute for therapy, counseling, or other professional mental health services. Participation in this workbook does not establish a therapist–client relationship. Although the author is a licensed mental health professional, this resource is offered in a non-clinical capacity. Readers are encouraged to seek support from a qualified mental health provider for personalized guidance and care.

First Paperback Edition: 2026

ISBN-13: 979-8-2189226-6-5

Cover design and typesetting by Melissa Williams Design.

Editorial and publishing support provided by Patella Publishing Services.

For information regarding bulk purchases, special sales, and more, please contact lisa@centeringtherapywellness.com.

Visit www.centeringtherapywellness.com for the latest updates and additional resources.

To my parents in heaven—

Thank you for shaping my path.
I would not be who I am, or where I am, without you.

Contents

DEAR READER,

You are taking a courageous step. One that signals you're ready to turn inward and listen to your own voice. You have reached your limit of how you currently live, and you're ready for change.

For many of us women, life has been a relentless cycle of working hard, keeping our heads down, grinding, and pushing forward without ever pausing to ask: What am I doing? Where am I going? Why am I living like this? What am I truly achieving?

I get it, I have lived that life too. For years I poured my energy into helping others. During an especially critical period, I cared for my aging parents while directing a mental health clinic. I was moving at full speed, from when I woke up to the time I laid my head on the pillow. I believed my worth was measured by how much I could give. But when my last parent passed, my world shifted. The busyness of one aspect of my life, which once filled a part of my days, vanished, leaving behind exhaustion, emptiness, and disconnection. In that stillness, I realized the way I had been living was unsustainable. I needed a change. There was no other way to get around this.

And so began my journey of being honest with myself and making hard decisions about my life. However, once I began to make these choices for change, the heaviness gradually lifted, and the path cleared. Through evidence-based tools, many grounded in Cognitive Behavioral Therapy (CBT), I transitioned from a state of survival to a more intentional and fulfilling way of living. Now, I'm here to share these tools with you.

My goal is to help you reconnect with yourself, gain clarity on what you want, and offer tools that can support you on your journey. Many of these tools I use with my clients, which have proven to support both mental health and personal growth. But more than that, they are practical and accessible, designed to meet you wherever you are in your life.

As you move through each of these chapters in their respective order, allow yourself to pause and to listen. Awareness is the first step toward transformation. If you need support along the way, reach out to a therapist, a coach, a trusted friend or family member. Above all, trust yourself. The most valuable guidance comes from within. This workbook is here to help you tune out the noise and rediscover the wisdom that already exists inside you.

Wherever you are on this journey, I am cheering you on. You are exactly where you need to be. And now, you get to choose where you go from here.

With deep gratitude,

Lisa Macedo, LMFT

CHAPTER 1

The Gift of Starting Again

Have you ever found yourself moving through the motions of your life but feeling strangely absent from it?

Between your career, family, and all your other responsibilities, you work hard to hold it all together. From the outside, people see you as strong, capable, and dependable. But inside, you feel flat. The things that once brought you joy don't light you up anymore. You keep pushing, telling yourself you'll rest when the list is done. But the list is never done!

And so you swing. Some days you're powering through at full speed, checking off boxes until late into the night. On other days, you collapse, unable to face one more task. You scroll through your phone, or you feel numb because you're too depleted to do anything else. You wonder, *Is this who I am now? Is the "real me" gone?*

If this feels familiar, I want you to know two things:

1. You are not alone.
2. This does not have to be your forever.

Why You're Here

You might not be using the word *burnout* yet. You just know that something is off. Life doesn't feel good anymore, and you can't keep living this way. You don't necessarily want to change everything about your life. In fact, most of what you have, you want to keep. But you do want to feel like yourself again: energized, present, and actually enjoying the life you've built.

That's why this workbook exists.

How to Use This Workbook

If you're picking up this workbook, chances are, you're running on fumes. And that's okay. You're here, and that's what matters most. This book is designed to help you take small, consistent steps toward feeling more grounded, energized, and in control of your life again.

The subsequent chapters are broken up into smaller segments. Each chapter includes instructions, insights, and tools to help you navigate this transition. Additionally, each chapter begins with a short story about a woman experiencing burnout. The chapter will conclude with final thoughts that summarize the main ideas presented throughout. In between, you will find these sections:

- **Reflection:** Ponder specific questions around your journey and journal your responses.
- **Challenge Activity:** Put into practice the tools shared to improve your life.
- **Chapter Action Items:** Track the activities you have completed.

These are places to specifically apply your learning and to mark up this workbook.

By completing this workbook, you will:

- Learn how to recognize the signs of burnout in your life;
- Understand how your thoughts, behaviors, and boundaries either fuel or heal burnout;
- Experiment with practical, evidence-based tools that will give you clarity and relief;
- Discover how to restore your energy and reintroduce joy into your daily routines; and
- Build a life that allows you not only to survive, but to thrive.

Through this workbook, you'll learn how to protect your energy, set healthier rhythms, and create space for what really matters. As a result, your life will become manageable and meaningful.

Take a Moment to Write It Down

This is not meant to be a passive experience. One of the biggest gifts of this workbook is getting thoughts out of your head and onto paper. Writing helps you to notice patterns, name what matters, and make your intentions real. As mentioned, throughout this workbook, there will be activities and exercises for you to capture your thoughts.

So, before you move on, try your first gentle assignment. Consider why you are here. Then write down your thoughts on these two questions:

- What motivated you to pick up this book today?

  ____

  ____

  ____

- What do you hope will feel different in your life when you finish this book?

  ____

  ____

  ____

How to Do This

When we're burned out, motivation is so incredibly fragile. Some days, even our best intentional, thought-out plans feel impossible. That's why we're going to use a simple Cognitive Behavioral Therapy (CBT) tool to help you achieve results. This skill is called activity scheduling.

Activity scheduling means making a plan to do certain activities at set times instead of waiting until you "feel like it." These activities can be anything: daily tasks, hobbies, anything you enjoy or that brings you a sense of accomplishment. By scheduling an activity, you're more likely to follow through. By doing the activity, you will lift your mood and break the cycle of procrastination.

So let's plan when you will use this workbook. Life happens, so the goal isn't perfection, but progress. By being intentional and writing out your goals, it makes it easier for you to remain committed, especially when motivation dips.

Plan Your Approach

Before diving in, take a few minutes to set yourself up for success:

How much time will you dedicate to this workbook each week? (5 min, 10 min, 30 min, 1 hour?) ______________________________

What days of the week would you like to read the workbook? (Pick days that are more realistic for you, days that you are less rushed and have room to pause and slow down.)

Let's add a checklist for the days of the week:

- ☐ Monday
- ☐ Tuesday
- ☐ Wednesday
- ☐ Thursday
- ☐ Friday
- ☐ Saturday
- ☐ Sunday

What time of day works best for you?

- ☐ Morning
- ☐ Afternoon
- ☐ Evening

Let's also think about how you will stay focused. Please mark what will work best for you:

If distractions creep in, I'll set myself up for success by:

__________ Putting my phone on Airplane Mode.

__________ Taking a quick movement break (walking, stretching, breathing).

__________ Creating a quiet space away from distractions to reset and refocus.

When you follow through on these small steps, you'll build self-trust and momentum—two powerful antidotes to burnout.

Know Your Why

Another CBT tool that helps us stay motivated is writing down our why. Now is a good time to consider the benefits of overcoming burnout.

Some examples may include:

- I want the energy to do the things I love.
- I want to enjoy my life instead of just survive it.
- I want to strengthen my relationships.
- I want to feel excited about learning and growing again.

You can write your reason below. You may also write your reasons on an index card or sticky note—or heck, a big whiteboard—and place it somewhere visible because we need all the motivation we can get right now. Read your reasons daily. Post it in your workstation, on the bathroom mirror, or on the cover of this book. Whenever motivation dips, let these reasons remind you why you're working through this book and why you want to beat burnout.

Advantages To Overcoming Burnout:

____

____

____

____

My Promise to You

As a therapist, I've worked with countless women who came to me in the exact place you are now: exhausted, joyless, overwhelmed, and unsure if change is even possible.

I specifically designed this workbook around the challenges women face in dealing with burnout. But burnout happens to everyone. The tools and strategies found in this book will benefit anyone who reads it. **Burnout happens to those of us who care deeply, have high expectations about ourselves, and give without boundaries.**

So I want you to learn what I now know:

The truth is . . . recovery isn't about doing *more*. It's about doing things *differently*. It's about small, intentional shifts that bring you back to yourself. And that is why I developed this workbook—so that you can discover and embrace this truth too.

Continue to show up and this workbook will walk with you as you learn how to pace your life in a way that recharges your energy and restores your joy.

At this point, there are three things I would like you to know:

1. Awareness is the start of every meaningful change. And you're here, which means you're aware that something needs to change.
2. Overcoming burnout isn't about throwing away your commitments or isolating yourself in order to recover. It's also not about muscling through and pretending exhaustion is normal. Instead, it's about finding a sustainable way forward, one where your energy, joy, and well-being matter just as much as your responsibilities. This workbook will help you do that.
3. Please know that every time you pick up this workbook, you're giving yourself a gift. You're inviting yourself to reclaim your energy, your joy, and your sense of self. And trust me, you are worth that gift.

In the next chapter, we'll look closely at the signs of burnout so you can recognize how it is showing up in your life. From there, I will guide you through the journey to recenter yourself—to reset your life so you can truly start living again.

CHAPTER 2

The Signs of Burnout

EMILY'S STORY

Emily stared blankly at her screen, unable to process what she was reading. For a couple of years, she had felt "off." It began when her company went through a reorg, and her new manager required longer hours to "hit" the ideal sales numbers for the year.

She worked hard but felt exhausted almost all the time. Joy was absent. She moved through her workday tasks like a machine, numbly completing projects and feeling detached from both her job and her personal life. Poor sleep compounded her exhaustion.

Her wake-up call came on a Saturday morning when she realized she didn't have the motivation to get out of bed. That moment pushed her to seek therapy. Based on the symptoms Emily shared, her therapist suggested she might be experiencing burnout. This had never occurred to Emily, and it helped give her clarity on why she was feeling this way.

The Signs of Burnout

Emily's story reflects classic burnout symptoms, and when you're in the middle of it, it's often difficult to recognize it yourself. You're still getting through your day, silently completing task after task, but there is a sense of detachment. You may also feel skeptical toward life. From the outside, people might never suspect you're struggling, mainly because even at your worst you're still producing quality work. However, this ability to "power through" can actually keep you trapped in a place of burnout.

While "burnout" became a buzzword during the COVID-19 pandemic, it's been recognized for decades. In 1974, psychotherapist and psychiatrist Herbert Freudenberger first introduced the term after observing volunteers in free health clinics, especially those supporting individuals struggling with addiction. In his article Staff Burn-Out (Journal of Social Issues, 1974), he described burnout as a state of emotional and physical exhaustion that happens when high expectations collide with disappointing or unmanageable outcomes. His research found that the most dedicated and committed people are often the most at risk.[1]

Although his focus was on helpers in crisis centers, his insight applies to many women today, especially caregivers, emotional anchors, and those doing invisible labor in their homes and communities. Freudenberger noted not only physical symptoms like fatigue and headaches, but also behavioral changes such as irritability, cynicism, and detachment.

Recent Research on Burnout

Today, burnout is recognized as more than just "being tired" or "stressed out." It is a systemic condition that impacts your body, mind, and relationships.

- Schaufeli & Enzmann define burnout as "a state of physical, emotional, and mental exhaustion caused by long-term involvement in situations that are emotionally demanding."[2]
- American Psychological Association (APA) Dictionary defines burnout as "physical, emotional, or mental exhaustion accompanied by decreased motivation, lowered performance, and negative attitudes toward oneself and others."[3]
- The National Institute for Occupational Safety and Health (NIOSH) refers to burnout as an "occupational phenomenon" caused by chronic workplace stress, emphasizing the need for both individual coping skills and systemic change.[4]

---

1 Herbert J. Freudenberger, "Staff Burn-Out," Journal of Social Issues 30, no. 1 (1974): 159–65.

2 Wilmar B. Schaufeli and Dieter Enzmann, The Burnout Companion to Study and Practice: A Critical Analysis (London: Taylor & Francis, 1998), 36.

3 American Psychological Association, s.v. "Burnout," APA Dictionary of Psychology, last modified April 19, 2018, https://dictionary.apa.org/burnout.

4 The National Institute for Occupational Safety and Health, "Module 2 Outline: What burnout is and is not," Centers for Disease Control and Prevention, last modified March 8, 2023, https://www.cdc.gov/niosh/learning/publichealthburnoutprevention/module-2/outline.html.

Burnout is a whole-body, whole-life shutdown. When I was at my peak burnout, my social world shrank, my sleep suffered, and my physical health declined because my energy reserves were so depleted.

This is why occasional self-care alone cannot "fix" burnout, especially when you're still living within a system, workplace, family, or culture that expects too much and gives too little. Women are often taught to push through, stay grateful, and keep going, even past the point of exhaustion.

Core Symptoms of Burnout

Widely accepted research identifies three primary symptoms:

1. Exhaustion
2. Cynicism
3. Feelings of ineffectiveness or lack of accomplishment

If you've felt like no amount of rest helps, if you find yourself emotionally pulling away from things that used to matter, or you find it harder to be effective, you may be experiencing burnout.

The good news: Burnout is not permanent. This workbook is designed to help you move from a numb, overwhelmed state to a more satisfying and balanced way of living.

Reflection: Symptoms of Burnout

After learning more about what burnout is and how it presents itself, take a moment to jot down your responses to the following questions:

- What symptoms related to burnout have you experienced or are currently experiencing?

  ____

  ____

  ____

- When did these symptoms first appear?

  ____

  ____

  ____

- How have these symptoms impacted your work, health, or personal relationships?

___

___

___

- Which aspects of your life or job do you believe contribute to these feelings?

___

___

___

Assessing Your Burnout Level

One widely used tool for measuring burnout is the **Maslach Burnout Inventory (MBI)**, developed by psychologist Christina Maslach and her colleagues. The MBI evaluates burnout across three dimensions:

- Emotional exhaustion
- Depersonalization (feeling disconnected from others or your work)
- Reduced personal accomplishment

If you'd like to assess your current burnout level, the Maslach Burnout Inventory (MBI) is available for individual purchase. Instructions for accessing the survey can be found in the Activity Resources section at the end of this book. After completion, you'll receive a personalized report to help you understand your results.[5]

You may also find you don't need a formal inventory to know where you stand, and that's okay. If you are aware that things feel off in your life, that is the most important thing in moving forward toward a life reset.

5 Christina Maslach, Susan E. Jackson, Michael P. Leiter, and Wilmar B. Schaufeli, "Individual Report: MBI-GS," Mind Garden, accessed December 19, 2025, https://www.mindgarden.com/mbi-general-survey/177-mbigs-individual-report.html.

(Optional) Challenge Activity: Burnout Inventory

If you're ready, consider completing the Maslach Burnout Inventory to establish a baseline. Although I have no affiliation with this assessment, I've seen the value it provides in creating a clear picture of where you are now and what can change as you work through this workbook.

Follow-Up Questions:

- What score did you get?

  ____

- Did the score surprise you? Why or why not?

  ____

  ____

- Any additional thoughts about your score?

  ____

  ____

Knowing your score can serve as an early warning system and help you track your recovery progress over time.

Burnout vs. Grief

Imagine Emily's story takes a turn. She's still ignoring the signs of burnout—pushing harder, resting less—when suddenly her mom is diagnosed with cancer.

Her calendar now fills with doctor's appointments and caregiving responsibilities, and suddenly, burnout and grief collide. Already depleted, Emily now faces the even greater emotional weight of what lies ahead layered on top of her daily burdens. Her exhaustion deepens, her clarity fogs, and her capacity shrinks.

Before we go further into this workbook, it's important to pause here and make a distinction. When we think of burnout, it is typically an overextension and ongoing chronic stress with work, school, or other duties. On the other hand, grief comes from a loss—such as a loved one, a pet, a job, or a relationship—which also requires acknowledgment and healing.

Worksheet Prompt: Burnout or Grief?

How do you know if the emptiness you feel is due to burnout or grief? Take a few minutes to answer these questions and reflect on your responses:

1. **What is the source of my exhaustion right now?**
   - Ongoing demands, overwork, or caregiving strain (Burnout)
   - Loss or major life change (Grief)
   - Both
2. **How do my emotions feel?**
   - Flat, numb, detached, irritable (Burnout)
   - Sad, longing, waves of pain or yearning (Grief)
3. **What brings me relief?**
   - Rest, boundaries, reduced workload (Burnout)
   - Talking, ritual, space to feel the loss (Grief)
4. **What do I need most right now?**
   - Energy restoration
   - Emotional support
   - Both

Recognizing whether you're experiencing burnout, grief, or both allows you to respond with the care you actually need. Sometimes that means reducing your workload. Other times it means giving yourself space to grieve. And sometimes, it means addressing both needs.

If you're reading this and neither burnout nor grief resonates with your experience, listen to that voice. Seek out mental health support for more clarity, understanding, and guidance tailored to what you are truly going through.

Chapter Action Items

- ☐ Identify your personal burnout symptoms.
- ☐ Try the **Challenge Activity: Burnout Inventory** (optional).
- ☐ Reflect on your results and insight (if applicable).
- ☐ Complete the **Worksheet Prompt: Burnout vs. Grief.**

FINAL THOUGHTS

Emily's burnout wasn't obvious to those around her, but naming it gave her language, clarity, and, most importantly, a starting point for change.

Like Emily, awareness is your first step toward healing. This chapter offers you tools to identify burnout in your own life, differentiate burnout from grief, and start recognizing burnout's deeper impact.

In the next chapter, we'll explore how burnout doesn't just affect your mind; it also shows up in your body. You'll learn to recognize the physical signals your nervous system sends when it's overwhelmed and how to respond with gentle, restorative care.

CHAPTER 3

The Nervous System and Burnout

SAMANTHA'S STORY

As her friend shared details about their upcoming weekend plans, Samatha's mind ping-ponged back and forth over her long list of to-do's and, physically, she felt restless. Five minutes later, she realized she did not hear one morsel of the story her friend shared. She wondered, *Why can't I be in the moment? Why am I so spaced out, frazzled, and distracted?*

Her frustration simmered. The night before, she had spent hours in the emergency room after her young son fell out of bed with excruciating arm pain. Thankfully, the hospital wasn't too busy, but after the X-rays and the MRI, it was 2:00 a.m. by the time they got home. Sleep was shallow and broken. Every time she stirred, she worried about him.

By morning, she pushed herself into work mode. Her heart raced. Her stomach churned. Her thoughts felt slow and heavy. Her body was in high gear, but her mind was crawling.

Then she remembered something she'd once read about: the 4-7-8 breathing technique (inhale for four seconds, hold for seven, exhale for eight). She decided to try it. At first it felt awkward. But after a few rounds, her chest loosened, her thoughts slowed, and she felt a small but meaningful shift toward clarity. The fog hadn't fully lifted, but there was enough space to focus on the present and the next step she needed to take.

Burnout and the Body

Have you ever experienced something similar to what Samantha went through? Where you wake up from an intense night and carry both the emotional weight and unexplained physical symptoms into the next day? You don't feel like yourself but you have an endless to-do list you can't pause, even if you feel strained and unsteady. I know I have had those days, and they are no fun!

When we experience burnout, our body is in a certain state that we most often are not aware of. Burnout isn't just emotional fatigue. It's a whole-body state. When we are under stress for long periods of time, our bodies turn everyday responsibilities into a threat. Our nervous system remains on high alert, as if danger is constantly looming. And while this heightened state of activation can help us power through urgent situations, over time it drains our bodies, fogs our minds, and makes recovery feel impossible. However, the beauty of our body is that there is a part of our system that helps us recover after we are in danger, and we have to learn to practice using that part.

To understand how burnout hijacks your body and how our body can recover from it, we need to take a look at the two key players in your autonomic nervous system: the **sympathetic nervous system** and the **parasympathetic nervous system.**

The Role of the Sympathetic & Parasympathetic Nervous Systems

Your sympathetic nervous system is like your body's emergency response team. I call this system the "stress system." It activates your *fight-or-flight* response by pumping out stress hormones such as cortisol and adrenaline, making you act. In short bursts, this system is helpful. But when it's constantly switched on, as it often is during burnout, it takes a damaging toll on your life.

In a true emergency, this response is life saving. But the problem is that many women live as if *every day is an emergency*—like they are in a war zone. We're constantly juggling work, caregiving, emotional labor, aging parents, social pressure, unspoken expectations, and more—and we rarely, if ever, pause.

Long-term sympathetic activation can lead to:

- Physical exhaustion
- Startle response
- Anxiety and irritability

- Brain fog
- Digestive issues
- Weakened immune function
- Mysterious illnesses

On the flip side, your parasympathetic nervous system is your rest-and-digest system. It slows your heart rate, supports digestion, and restores balance after stressful events. In parasympathetic mode, you feel grounded, present, and safe, like those moments right before sleep when your breath deepens and your belly rises and falls.

In burnout, the sympathetic system dominates, trapping you in a cycle of tension and fatigue, even when you try to rest. Your mind keeps racing. Your shoulders stay tight. Relaxation feels out of reach.

My Story: Living in "High Alert"

In my own life, I spent years in constant sympathetic activation. Every task felt urgent. My cortisol and adrenaline levels ran high, giving me bursts of energy, leaving me wired then depleted at the end of each day. I remember startling easily—even when someone simply said hello—because my body was primed to see everything as a potential threat.

Many nights, I left work and headed straight to the ICU, or another wing of the hospital, to support my parents. Looking back, this was relentless on my nervous system. My "normal" was me stuck in a tense sympathetic state, but this is not a safe place to dwell in. For years, I remained in this unhealthy state of survival.

That's why burnout recovery isn't just mental. It's physical. Your body must relearn safety before it can rest, restore, and heal.

The Power of Burnout Recovery

Yes, burnout recovery is a thing. It is the process of guiding your mind and body out of survival mode and into a state where energy, clarity, and joy can return. It's not instant. It's not linear. But it's absolutely possible.

Through burnout recovery, you can:

- Experience genuine rest;
- Feel excitement about your day;
- Rekindle joy and passion;
- Find fulfillment and purpose; and
- Restore a sense of balance and control.

And you deserve every single one of these outcomes. For many women, we have spent years pushing our bodies when we are receiving signals to slow down. We've trained our body to survive in constant alert. But it's time to change that.

Now that you have an understanding of the two systems that activate while in stress and recovery, the sympathetic and parasympathetic nervous systems, let's move into some tools that will help you with your burnout recovery plan. First, it's important you understand your body and its response to your current life.

Reflection: Body Check-In

Take a moment to gently check in with your body and mind. Consider these questions and write down your response.

- How does your body typically respond to stress or overwhelm?

  ____

  ____

  ____

- Can you recall a time when your nervous system felt stuck in "high alert"? What do you remember about how your body responded?

  ____

  ____

  ____

How to Regulate Your Stress Response

You don't have to stay stuck in fight-or-flight mode. There are simple, effective practices that can help shift your body into parasympathetic activation and support your recovery.

Here are several science-backed techniques you can begin using right away to interrupt the sympathetic system. These CBT tools offer mindfulness and stress-management support that engage your parasympathetic system.

Tools to Regulate and Heal Your Body

1. **Deep, Slow Breathing**

   Diaphragmatic (belly) breathing slows the breath, quiets the mind, and signals safety to the body. The 4-7-8 technique—inhale for four seconds, hold for seven, exhale for eight—is one powerful deep breathing option.

2. **Progressive Muscle Relaxation (PMR)**

   Tense muscles then slowly relax those muscles. This helps release built-up tension and guides your body from a state of stress to rest. This can be practiced by clenching your fists for five seconds and then relaxing them for five seconds. You can also do this with other areas of the body: feet, calves, eyes, lips! This technique will disrupt your stress system, giving you awareness and pulling you out of your tense sympathetic state.

3. **Gentle Movement**

   Activities like yoga, stretching, or a slow walk in nature can pull your body out of high-alert mode. These movements send signals that you're no longer in danger, which then allows your body to begin to relax. Too busy? Think of small time commitments. Taking 5 minutes to do a YouTube yoga stretch can quickly shift yourself to a more grounded state. Or a two-minute walk can change your internal world.

4. **Grounding Exercises**

   Reconnecting to your surroundings is another simple way to regulate your nervous system. Use the 5-4-3-2-1 method:

   - 5 things you see
   - 4 things you can touch
   - 3 things you hear
   - 2 things you smell
   - 1 thing you taste

This sensory awareness practice brings you back into the present moment, which helps calm the nervous system and reduces the feeling of threat.

5. **Connection & Laughter**

   Talk to a friend, cuddle a pet, or watch something funny. Human connection and joy are powerful antidotes to stress. These acts instantly engage your parasympathetic system.

Small Steps to Rebalance

Burnout recovery is not a quick fix, but these techniques start the process to rewire your nervous system. Each of these only takes a few minutes a day—just small, daily shifts of deep breathing before bed, stretching in the morning, or stepping outside in the sunlight. These little efforts will go a long way toward healing your body.

Challenge Activity: Slowing Down

Now that we understand how to activate our parasympathetic nervous system, let's try it out! Choose one of the tools listed. Try it out. After, record how your body feels:

- What technique did you try?

  ____

  ____

  ____

- How did your body feel afterward?

  ____

  ____

  ____

Actively practicing these tools helps heal the body. Commit to making this challenge a routine for yourself. By making it a part of your day, you give your parasympathetic nervous system a daily hug!

Chapter Action Items

- ☐ Complete the **Reflection: Body Check-In.**
- ☐ Try the **Challenge Activity: Slowing Down.**
- ☐ Reflect on the effects.

FINAL THOUGHTS

It's important to recognize that burnout doesn't just live in the mind—it also lives in the body. When the sympathetic nervous system is constantly activated, it keeps us in a heightened state of alert, draining our energy, resilience, and capacity to recover. This chapter underscores the truth that the body and mind are deeply interconnected. When your nervous system is stuck in overdrive, rest doesn't come easily, and we feel out of touch with life and ourselves.

However, you have the power to shift this at any moment by activating the parasympathetic nervous system. Through simple, intentional practices, like deep breathing, progressive muscle relaxation, grounding exercises, and pausing for moments of connection, you begin to regulate your nervous system. Use these tools at any time. They help bring your body out of survival mode and into a state where healing is truly possible.

As you retrain your nervous system to feel safe again, you will feel a positive shift in energy, clarity, and calmness. Remember, you are capable of creating change at any moment—and within each of these moments, you bring yourself a step closer to recovering from burnout.

CHAPTER 4

Learning Who We Are

KELSEY'S STORY

Kelsey is in her fifties, and she always has been the reliable one at work, in her family, and in her community. She's a senior manager at a nonprofit, where she's worked for over twenty years. Everyone counts on her to keep things running.

But lately, each morning, she dreads opening her laptop. Her calendar is packed with back-to-back meetings, and even though she rarely takes time off, she feels like she's constantly falling behind. At night she lies in bed, replaying conversations and to-do lists, and in the morning, she hits the snooze button over and over. She used to feel passionate about her work, but now it feels like she's just going through the motions.

Her weekends aren't a break. They're spent catching up on laundry, managing her kids and her aging parents' appointments, and responding to "just one more thing" from her team. Even when she's technically off, she can't relax. Her mind races, her jaw stays clenched, and her body feels like it's on high alert.

When friends ask how she's doing, she says "fine," but inside she's running on empty. Kelsey is starting to wonder "*When did caring for others start costing me this much?*" She isn't sad, exactly. She's just exhausted in a way that rest alone doesn't seem to fix.

Eventually, Kelsey tries something simple. She tracks her mood and energy levels every day. At first it feels strange, but soon she starts noticing patterns: what drained her, what gave her a spark, and what keeps leaving her feeling flat. That small act of observation becomes a turning point, giving her the clarity to make more intentional choices about where her time and energy goes.

Why Your Energy Feels "Random" (But it Isn't)

What Kelsey is experiencing is classic burnout. She is overextending herself, feeling exhausted, and is not sure what makes her feel this way. I've seen this shift in mood and energy with clients. If you are experiencing burnout, then you, too, have probably felt waves of different emotions and energy. One moment you feel motivated, and the next completely drained. You chalk it up to "just a random day."

The truth is, these shifts aren't random at all. They're often early signals of burnout tied to specific triggers and patterns in your daily life. In fact, the three core symptoms of burnout—**exhaustion, cynicism, and a sense of ineffectiveness**—can each rise and fall throughout your day, depending on what you're doing, who you're with, and how you're feeling. Sometimes even procrastination is a clue that one of these symptoms is spiking.

When we start tracking our days, we can see these patterns clearly. And with clarity comes the power to make small, intentional changes that have a big impact.

Becoming a Scientist in Your Own Life

Like Kelsey, you can learn to spot the connection between your daily experiences and your energy level. This chapter is about transformation through gathering information.

Think of yourself as a scientist—observing, taking notes, and looking for patterns. Kelsey didn't just "push through" her exhaustion anymore; she got curious about it. Which meetings left her drained? Which tasks gave her energy? Which people lifted her up or pulled her down? Over time, she could see exactly what fueled her burnout and what supported her well-being.

This is especially important for women because we've often been taught to care for everyone else before ourselves. But here, this observation is about you and understanding what makes you feel the way you do.

Challenge Activity: Monitor Your Symptoms

One of the most effective tools we can use from CBT is monitoring your symptoms. Just like you might track your spending or your workouts, you will want to track daily how often you notice the three key burnout symptoms: exhaustion, cynicism, and a sense of ineffectiveness.

The Daily Sumptom-Monitoring Sheet

Directions:

Every night, for a month, rate your three core burnout symptoms on a scale from **0–10** (0 = not present at all, 10 = at the extreme level). Then complete the reflection questions to increase your awareness of patterns.

Ratings:

- My Exhaustion level today (0–10): ________
- My Cynicism (pessimism, irritability, or loss of empathy) level today (0–10): ________
- My Ineffectiveness/Lack of Accomplishment level today (0–10): ________

If you monitor your symptoms for a month, **(use what is practical to you, the notes app of your phone, a notebook)** you will discover patterns that otherwise you might miss. These patterns will become your roadmap for change.

Reflection: Notice Your Symptoms

What did you notice today about your exhaustion, cynicism, and feelings of ineffectiveness? Write down your observations:

1. Did your **exhaustion** go up or down? What were you doing? Who were you with?

   ____

   ____

   ____

2. How about your **cynicism**? What increased or decreased it today?

____

3. Did you feel **ineffective** in your work or day-to-day tasks? What helped or hurt?

4. Did you learn anything new with tracking these symptoms?

5. Can you identify what might prevent these symptoms from changing?

Reminder: *The more you track, the more you'll notice, and awareness is the first step toward real, lasting change.*

Chapter Action Items

- ☐ Complete the **Challenge Activity: Monitor Your Symptoms.**
- ☐ Answer the questions in **Reflection: Notice Your Symptoms.**

FINAL THOUGHTS

In this chapter, you became a scientist of your own life. You brought out a microscope and, intentionally and nonjudgmentally, checked in with yourself to know more about your energy, frustration, cynicism, and productivity. Monitoring your symptoms is a powerful CBT tool that shows us which thoughts help or hurt us.

Over time, this daily insight will protect your energy, empower you to set boundaries, and guide you into parts of life that replenish you.

In the next chapters, we will explore additional CBT tools that can pull you closer to the recovery you desire.

CHAPTER 5

The Power of Our Beliefs

AMANDA'S STORY

Amanda wakes up at 7:00 a.m. Her ritual is to start her day with writing out her "to-do" list. This list is compiled with every facet of her life—and I mean everything! From unfinished emails, back-to-back work meetings, her exercise schedule, personal errands, household chores, activities within her big professional project that always feel incomplete—each task piles up on her "to-do" list.

Every morning she tells herself, *"I have to get this all done today, or tomorrow will be beyond stressful."*

This is her routine.

She stretches herself very thin to check off as much as she can before the end of her night. But when she does, she gets annoyed that it's not all done. She goes to bed exhausted.

On the days when she does get the full list complete, she feels accomplished, and views the day as "a good day." Finally, she can relax. But when she turns on the TV, she is so drained she can hardly keep track of the show. Instead, she is busy thinking about what she needs to do tomorrow. She is never able to fully relax.

How Our Beliefs Contribute to Burnout

What Amanda doesn't realize yet is that her depletion isn't just from the tasks: It's from the belief driving them, the belief that her worth depends on finishing the list.

I have worked with many clients who have similarly encountered feelings of exhaustion and disconnection in all parts of their life because their long-standing belief is that they "first have to get everything done before there is time to pause."

Many of us, including myself, carry silent rules we never originally agreed to. These rules often sound like:

- Be helpful.
- Don't complain.
- Do it all and make it look easy.
- Productivity equals worthiness.

These beliefs can originate from a variety of different places in our lives. In homes, cultures, and society we see values placed around our high level of productivity. The call to achieve comes with greater regard than our call for peace.

Do you find yourself:

- Constantly pushing past your limits?
- Unable to rest without feeling guilt?
- Tying your worth to how much you achieve?

If so, there is a solid reason for this. It's tied to the messages you keep sending yourself, and this chapter will help you look at your behavior and unlearn some of those beliefs that are keeping you stuck in a burnout cycle.

How CBT Helps Us Shift Our Beliefs

Cognitive Behavioral Therapy (CBT) shows us how thoughts, feelings, and behaviors are interconnected.

Our thoughts influence our emotions, and those emotions shape our behaviors. This cycle, called the *cognitive triangle,* is a basic visual of CBT.

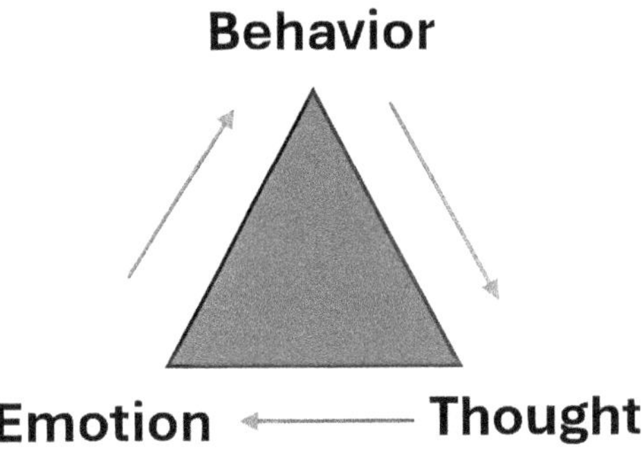

Let's use an example to bring this to life: Let's say I believe *"I don't deserve to rest until everything is done"* (which was a strong belief of mine!). This means anytime I feel a need to relax when I have things to get done, my thoughts trigger a sense of anxiety. To counter this anxiety, I demonstrate behavior of pushing myself to move faster, to get more and more things done from my "to-do" list, even though my body is telling me it is exhausted. And that cycle? It's what fuels burnout. For me, I was a machine. I got everything (for the most part) done. I answered texts, emails, and calls at all hours. I truly confused productivity with worth, and exhaustion with achievement.

So how does CBT help? It can invite us to question the beliefs beneath our thoughts, emotions, and behavior, and then decide whether these beliefs still deserve to guide our lives. If we want to change our behavior, we need to go to the source and change our beliefs.

Three Steps to Shift a Belief

How we shift our beliefs comes down to three important steps:

Step 1: Identify the Limiting Belief

Limiting beliefs are the unspoken rules we live by. Often these beliefs are inherited, unexamined, or rooted in fear. Example: *"I don't deserve to rest until everything is done."*

These deeper beliefs aren't obvious at first. They show up as quick, automatic thoughts like "I should keep working" or "I can't relax yet."

To uncover the belief behind the thought, we use a process called **guided discovery.** In CBT, this is also known as the "downward arrow technique."

Start with a recent situation that triggered stress, guilt, or self-criticism. Then reflect on these questions:

- "What was going through my mind right before I felt that way?"
- "If that thought were true, what would it mean about me?"
- "What would it say about me if I didn't do this?"
- "What am I afraid might happen if I didn't follow this rule?"

As you keep asking, your answers will move from surface thoughts to deeper assumptions or rules (like "I must finish everything before I rest") to the core belief underneath (like "I don't deserve rest unless I've earned it").

Once you've identified that deeper belief, you can examine where it comes from, how it affects you, and whether it truly serves you today.

Step 2: Challenge the Belief

Our brains like to treat limiting beliefs as facts, but they're not: They're assumptions. And assumptions can be questioned.

Ask yourself:

- "What do I gain by believing this? What do I lose?" This is called the **cost-benefit analysis** in CBT.
- "Is it always true that I must finish everything before resting?"
- "Was there ever a time when resting before finishing everything turned out fine?" Challenging a belief is called **Socratic questioning** in CBT.
- "Can I change the way I think about rest and responsibility so that it's more balanced?" This is called the **straight-forward technique** in CBT.

In challenging your belief, you might discover that your "to-do" list is never-ending, that it regenerates daily. You might also discover that pushing through exhaustion actually reduces your focus, creativity, and emotional regulation. In fact, you might even recognize that your worth isn't earned by how much you do. Instead, your rest allows you to get through that "to do" list with greater thoughtfulness.

Step 3: Replace with a Balanced Belief

Changing a belief isn't about swinging to the other extreme. Rather you are seeking a healthy belief, or a balanced belief. This is about finding a middle ground by asking questions like, "Can I look at this belief in another way?"

A healthier belief might be:

- *"I am responsible, but that doesn't mean I need to be perfect or do everything at once. I may not finish everything today, and that's okay. I can continue tomorrow."*

These are beliefs grounded in truth, and which support sustainable well-being.

Challenge Activity: Shift a Belief

Now you try:

What belief do you have that fuels your burnout?

____

____

____

How can you challenge and reframe this belief in a way that serves you better?

____

____

____

If this reframed belief resonates with you, make sure to use it when your original belief pops up—and believe me, it will. This is not a one-and-done change. Like most things, we need to practice using our framed beliefs every day in order to see changes in our behavior.

Nature & Nurture: Where Our Beliefs Begin

Nature: What We Inherit

If mental health conditions like anxiety, depression, or Attention Deficit Hyperactivity Disorder run in your family, they can influence how you respond to pressure. Challenges like difficulty regulating emotions, perfectionism, or avoidance may not just be personality quirks: They might have biological roots. And when left unaddressed, these traits can increase your risk for burnout.

In the absence of healthy coping mechanisms, many of us turn to what we *know as a way to manage*: overworking, overachieving, or numbing ourselves with busyness. These are often unconscious responses—habits developed as ways to feel safe, seen, or in control.

For me, I learned later in life, as I learned more about mental health, that anxiety ran strong in my family. This was a strong generational pattern that helped me understand more about why things affected me so much more. With great therapists, friends, and friends who are therapists, I was able to take care of myself and start living the life that I wanted to live.

Understanding the role of your genetic predispositions isn't about blame. It's about awareness, so you can respond with compassion and care, instead of criticism and shame.

Reflection: Your Genetic Disposition

Consider these questions. Capture your thoughts in the lines below.

1. When you think about the emotional patterns in your family—worry, avoidance, irritability, over-responsibility, or perfectionism—what parallels do you notice in yourself today?

   ____
   ____
   ____

2. How have these inherited tendencies helped you in certain seasons of your life, and in what ways have they made things harder?

   ____
   ____
   ____

3. Knowing what you now understand about your genetic and family patterns, what is one gentle shift you'd like to make to support your well-being moving forward?

   ____

   ____

   ____

Bringing these genetic dispositions into the light allows you to start shifting them. And that's where healing begins.

Nurture: What We Learned Growing Up

Earlier, I mentioned how some of our beliefs are inherited. Our upbringing plays a powerful role in shaping how we see our lives, how we view our work, our rest, and our worth. For example, if you grew up in a home where positive reinforcement was tied to productivity and achievement, it makes sense that slowing down feels wrong to you now.

Growing up with immigrant parents from the Azores Islands, I saw hard work modeled every day. I was also praised when I was dedicated, self-sacrificing, and perseverant. I learned that the more I did, the more I was positively validated. As a result, I ran my world with some of these unhealthy beliefs for years:

If I do more, maybe people will appreciate me.

- I'll make people happy if I overextend myself.
- I don't deserve to take time for myself.
- I can only rest once everything is done on my list.

These beliefs drained me. However, I believed that people loved this Lisa. Meanwhile, the harder I pushed, the more depleted I became, until eventually, my body forced me to stop.

But it truly wasn't until after my mother passed, when her appointments ended and the house grew quiet, that the full weight of everything hit me. Grief and burnout didn't just sit beside me, they wrapped around me like a heavy blanket. Even the smallest tasks felt impossible. Every decision, every step, felt like wading through quicksand. I spent more weekends in bed than I care to admit, just trying to summon the energy to move, to exercise, to feel like myself again.

And yet, despite my deep love for my work as a therapist and Clinical Director, I couldn't ignore what I was seeing in the mirror: This wasn't the life I wanted. And it certainly wasn't the life I encouraged my clients, or the therapists I trained, to live.

Reflection: Your Beliefs

Now it's your turn. Reflect on your beliefs by answering these questions:

- What messages did my family tell or model to me about work and rest?

  ____

  ____

  ____

- When was I praised? When was I criticized?

  ____

  ____

  ____

- How did that shape my beliefs about worth?

  ____

  ____

  ____

Work Beliefs

- Do I feel more worthy when I'm productive?

  ____

  ____

  ____

- What would happen if I did less but still earned the same?

  ____

  ____

  ____

Rest Beliefs

- Do I feel guilty when I rest? Why?

____
____
____

- What other emotions surface when I slow down?

____
____
____

Self-Worth Beliefs

- What do I believe makes a person worthy?

____
____
____

- What would I tell a friend who believed the same thing?

____
____
____

The Power of a Mantra

My unhealthy beliefs drove me into a state of burnout until I replaced them with new, more balanced beliefs. My mantra became:

"I deserve a break no matter what's left on my list. I can move with ease and energy."

It wasn't instant. The old version of me—Lisa 1.0—still pops up, urging me to push harder. But with practice, I learned to pause, notice, and choose differently.

Challenge Activity: Create an Empowering Mantra

Now create your own mantra:

1. Identify a belief that no longer serves you.
2. Imagine your best friend saying it. What would you tell them?
3. Reframe it into a supportive mantra here:
    - ______________________________
    - ______________________________
    - ______________________________

Now wear it loud! Put it on a sticky note, sing it in the shower, or repeat it before bed. At the end of the day, journal your observations. How did you feel living by this mantra?

____

____

____

Just a reminder that none of this works overnight. These tools take time to settle in and actually create lasting change. The goal is to practice this mantra every day. Recovery is a process—not a quick fix. With consistent effort, your thoughts, emotions, and behaviors will shift, and over time you'll build new beliefs that support you and make your life fuller and stronger.

Chapter Action Items

- ☐ Reframe a belief through the **Challenge Activity: Shift a Belief.**
- ☐ Complete **Reflection: Your Genetic Disposition.**
- ☐ Complete **Reflection: Your Beliefs.**
- ☐ Identify a limiting belief and complete **Challenge Activity: Create an Empowering Mantra.**

FINAL THOUGHTS

You just took a big step by learning to see how your beliefs lead to your burnout. By understanding the patterns you are in, you can now choose differently. When you notice a belief that drains you, pause and ask: *"Do I want to keep this belief, or is there a kinder, truer one to guide me?"*

By creating mantras that serve you, you are in the driver's seat to change your life. At any point in your journey, you can steer away from harmful, false beliefs and consciously head down the path that will allow you to reach a better version of you.

CHAPTER 6

The Emotional Math of Burnout: Guilt and Shame

JESSICA'S STORY

Jessica was a thirty-six-year-old stay-at-home mom of two young kids. Her days were filled with snacks, laundry, pickups, tantrums, and bedtime stories. She loved her children deeply, and staying home with them was a conscious decision she and her partner had made together. But guilt seemed to hover over everything.

Last week, Jessica had asked her mom to babysit for a few hours so she could go to a yoga class and grab a quiet coffee afterward. She had been feeling run-down, emotionally drained, and mentally foggy, but when she sat alone in the café, she didn't feel relief. Instead, she felt guilt.

"*What kind of mom chooses yoga and coffee over her kids?*" she thought. "*Other moms do this all day without needing a break.*"

The guilt turned into shame. She wondered if she just wasn't cut out for this. Maybe she was too selfish. Maybe she wasn't a good mom after all.

By the time she got home, her body was still tense and her mind raced with self-judgment. Her break away from her kids had been swallowed by an inner narrative that she didn't deserve the break in the first place.

Later that night, Jessica noticed the heaviness of her guilt and how deeply she felt like she wasn't a good enough wife, mom, or even person. She remembered her friend once saying that the way we talk to ourselves can reinforce guilt and shame, and that "should" statements often fuel that inner critic. It's like we're constantly "should-ing" on ourselves. So, Jessica paid attention to those messages and slowly shifted the tone. Instead of saying, "I shouldn't need this," she told herself, "I wish I were the Energizer Bunny, but I'm human. I need a break from my life sometimes, and that helps restore me so I can be more present with my family." It wasn't a magic fix, but it chipped away the guilt and shame she carried with her.

Identifying Ingrained Patterns

Maybe you've caught yourself thinking thoughts similar to Jessica's, wondering whether you're allowed to rest, doubting whether you're doing enough, or comparing yourself to some imaginary version of a "better" woman.

When it comes to managing burnout, two of the most common emotional blocks I hear from my clients are guilt and shame. Over and over, I hear phrases like:

- "I should be working more."
- "I shouldn't need a break."
- "I feel guilty for not going to my child's_______ (event)."
- "I feel guilty going out with my friends because I'm not with my children."

These statements are examples of **"should statements"**—self-imposed rules or expectations about how we *should* act, feel, or perform. While they may feel like guidance, they often create pressure, self-criticism, and anxiety. Constantly telling ourselves what we "should" do can amplify guilt and shame, making us feel like we're never enough.

These aren't just fleeting thoughts; they are deeply ingrained patterns that drain us emotionally, mentally, and physically. When we don't talk about shame and guilt, we reinforce the cultural script that women must hold it together and carry on with a smile while quietly feeling depleted.

I also hear many women say, *"Other mothers are able to handle more than I can. What's wrong with me?"* This is one of the most heartbreaking beliefs I hear, and it is a total lie. It speaks to how shame convinces us we are defective for simply being human.

The reality is that needing a break—whether it's five minutes, five days, or five years—is being human. And the perception that we must always act like we have our lives perfectly together is a damaging social narrative impacting the well-being of today's women.

Research shows that shame is associated with increased stress, rumination, and avoidance behaviors, all of which increase the risk of burnout.[1] Additionally, guilt—especially maladaptive guilt, which is not tied to wrongdoing—can increase psychological distress and make it harder to engage in necessary self-care.[2] Because of the negative impact shame and guilt can have on our mental health, we will dive deeper and distinguish these feelings further in the section below.

The Role of Shame and Guilt in Burnout

Let's define the difference in simple terms:

- **Guilt** is the feeling that you did something wrong. It usually shows up when your actions don't match your values.
- **Shame** is deeper. It's the feeling that there's something wrong with you—as if you, at your core, are not good enough.

Examples of Guilt Thoughts:

- "I should be focusing on my kids or the housework at all times."
- "I'm not doing enough for my family."

Examples of Shame Thoughts:

- "I should be able to manage all of this. I feel so alone in what I'm feeling."
- "If people saw the real me, they would know I don't have it together."

---

1 June Price Tangney and Ronda L. Dearing, *Shame and Guilt* (New York: The Guilford Press, 2002), 52-60, 112-120.

2 Jane Bybee, Rolande Merisca, and Rashid Velasco, "The Development of Reactions to Guilt-Producing Events," in *Guilt and Children*, ed. Jane Bybee (San Diego: Academic Press, 1998), 185–213.

Reflection: Shame and Guilt

Pause to answer these questions.

1. **When have you felt guilt recently?**

___

___

___

How did you respond?

___

___

___

Did it lead to helpful action, or did it just drain you?

___

___

___

2. **Does shame show up in your self-talk?**

___

___

___

In those moments, what does your inner voice say about you?

___

___

___

How do those thoughts affect your relationships or daily life?

___

___

___

Challenge the "Should" Statements

A common source of guilt and shame are these "should" statements. These self-imposed rules or expectations about how we *should* act, feel, or perform create cognitive distortion and an automatic pattern of thinking that hold us to unrealistic or rigid standards.

Examples of "Should" Statements:

- "I should be more productive."
- "I should be able to do it all."
- "I shouldn't need help."
- "I should be focusing on my family at all times."

Don't these statements sound like rules? But whose rules are they? They are often not our own but come from voices we've absorbed from our culture, family, or social expectations.

Reframing them softens their power. For example:

- "It would be nice if I was more productive."
- "I wish I didn't need the help, but I do."
- "It's okay to need rest."
- "Needing help doesn't make me weak. It makes me real."

This shift may seem small, but it's powerful. It creates breathing room for a more supportive inner dialogue.

Challenge Activity: "Should" Statements

Take a moment to notice any "shoulds" you have been carrying in the back of your mind lately. Write down 3–5 of them below.

____

____

____

____

____

____

Then ask yourself:

- Whose voice is this really? Is it mine, or does it come from a parent, teacher, society, or an old belief?

  ___
  ___
  ___

- Is this "should" statement helpful or harmful? Does it motivate me, or does it leave me feeling ashamed or inadequate?

  ___
  ___
  ___

- What can I say instead? Reframe the statement with kindness and truth.

  E.g., Replace "I should be more productive" with "I'm doing my best, and rest is productive, too."

  ___
  ___
  ___

Remember, awareness is the first step to breaking free from guilt and shame.

Write it Down

One powerful way to handle these thoughts is by using a thought record, a cognitive behavioral tool that helps you recognize and challenge unhelpful thinking patterns. When we write a thought down and see it on paper, it often lands differently than when it's just in our heads.

It helps to write down the guilt/shame thought, then look at the evidence for or against this thought, as if you're presenting your case in front of a judge.

The idea of this technique is to create a balanced thought.

Here is an example of an Examine The Evidence table used to help capture the evidence for and against a negative thought.

<table>
<tr><td colspan="2">Negative Thought:</td></tr>
<tr><td>Evidence For:</td><td>Evidence Against:</td></tr>
<tr><td></td><td></td></tr>
<tr><td colspan="2">Balanced Thought:</td></tr>
</table>

So, for example, you've just had a recurring thought: "I'm a bad mom because I missed the school event." Now:

1. Write it down.
2. Examine the evidence for this thought.
3. Examine the evidence against this thought.
4. Capture the balanced thought.

Here is a completed table showing the process to reach the balanced thought.

Negative Thought: *I'm a bad mom because I missed the event.*	
Evidence For	**Evidence Against**
I didn't make it to the event. My child was disappointed that I wasn't there.	I show up for my kids every day in other ways. I care for them daily, support their education, and love them deeply. Missing one event doesn't define my entire role as a mom. My child is learning that sometimes plans don't work out, and that doesn't mean they are unloved. One event does not erase all the positive moments and support I provide.
Balanced Thought: *Missing one event does not define my parenting. I care deeply about my child, and I show up in many meaningful ways. I can feel disappointed and still be a good mom.*	

Let's go through another example:

Negative Thought: *I should be able to do it all: work, cook, clean, volunteer, and still have energy for my kids. If I can't, I'm failing.*	
Evidence For	**Evidence Against**
I can't keep up with everything on my to-do list. I see other moms juggle work, volunteering, caring for their kids, and maintaining their own social connections.	No one can do everything perfectly all the time. I just don't see other moms' struggles. The standard I hold myself to may be unrealistic or even harmful. My kids benefit more from my presence and connection than from a perfectly clean house. Asking for help or saying no to extra commitments doesn't make me a failure; it models healthy boundaries.
Balanced Thought: *I can prioritize what matters most. My worth as a mom isn't measured by how much I get done.*	

Challenge Activity: Write and Balance a Guilt/Shame-Based Thought

Now you try. Pick one thought that makes you feel guilt or shame:

Step 1: Record this negative thought.

Step 2: Examine and record the evidence that supports this thought.

Step 3: Examine and record the evidence that goes against this thought.

Step 4: Based on the evidence of both sides from above, what is a more balanced thought you can write, that you believe blends the two sides?

Negative Thought:	
Evidence For:	**Evidence Against:**
Balanced Thought:	

Now practice catching these harmful thoughts. Create a table and write them down. Then work on the evidence, and challenge yourself to create more neutral thoughts. The more we practice this, the better we feel. Each improved thought is a step toward changing our narrative of who we are in this world.

Chapter Action Items

- ☐ Answer the questions in **Reflection: Shame and Guilt.**
- ☐ Try the **Challenge Activity: "Should" Statements.**
- ☐ Practice with the **Challenge Activity: Write and Balance a Guilt/Shame-Based Thought.**

FINAL THOUGHTS

Guilt and shame are natural human emotions, but they don't need to run the show. By naming them, working with them, and building compassionate practices, we loosen their grip. They move from the driver's seat to the back seat.

This shift in inner dialogue builds a stronger, more sustainable you and brings you closer to healing burnout.

CHAPTER 7

Boundaries: The Burnout Buster No One Talks About

LEAH'S STORY

Leah poured 100 percent of her energy into everything she did—at home, at work, in her relationships. She loved making other people's lives easier and said yes in every aspect of her life. People knew they could count on her. At work, she showed up, delivered, and was consistent through and through. At home, her kids were the light of her life, and she managed their extracurriculars while supporting her husband's demanding executive role. She also always made time to connect with her family and friends.

Although Leah loved much of what she did, she rarely had time to recharge. Her days became lists to conquer rather than experiences to enjoy. With little space for herself, she often felt depleted.

One day, Leah hit a wall. Something had to change. So, when someone asked her to take on another task, she tried something new. Instead of saying yes immediately, she paused and said she'd get back to them in twenty-four hours.

It felt strange and unfamiliar, but she reminded herself that always saying yes wasn't working anymore. That small pause gave her space to reflect: *Is this something I truly value? Do I have room for it on my already overflowing plate?*

That pause instigated a powerful shift. It reminded her that she could still be thoughtful and helpful without being endlessly available.

Why Boundaries Matter

Do you often say yes more than no, like Leah? Do you enjoy helping others, but feel drained because you're not caring for yourself? If so, you're like many women who are burnt out. With my clients experiencing burnout, these women tend to be so busy accommodating others, they neglect their own needs. This is a classic example of overexertion and poor boundaries with others.

The word "boundary" is the pop culture word of the year, and we hear it everywhere. But what does it really mean?

At their core, boundaries are the limits we set to protect our time, energy, and emotional well-being. Psychologist Dr. Henry Cloud, coauthor of *Boundaries*, defines them as personal property lines that clarify where you end and where others begin. Boundaries help you take ownership of your needs, responsibilities, and inner peace. They don't make life harder: They make it easier by giving us clear limits.[1]

Research consistently shows that strong boundaries support better mental health, reduce stress, and prevent burnout. One study in *The Journal of Occupational Health Psychology* found that people who maintained clear lines between work and personal life experienced lower stress, higher job satisfaction, and significantly less emotional exhaustion.[2]

On the flip side, weak or nonexistent boundaries often lead to chronic stress, resentment, and eventually burnout. When we fail to create space for ourselves, we disappear into the demands of everyone else.

I can attest to this personally. For years, I led with a "can-do" attitude, always saying yes before considering how it would affect me. Each request came with a dopamine hit with every thank-you. But thinking about others while ignoring myself eventually led me straight into burnout. The truth was, the only person who could dig me out of that hole was me.

The Invisible Weight

This struggle doesn't exist in a vacuum; it's woven into our culture. The women's movement has brought incredible progress, including access to careers, more

---

1 Henry Cloud and John Sims Townsend, *Boundaries: When to Say Yes, How to Say No, to Take Control of Your Life* (Grand Rapids, MI: Zondervan, 1992), 31.

2 June P. Tangney, Ronda L. Dearing, and Darlene L. Wagner, "Shame and Guilt in Adaptive and Maladaptive Self-Evaluations," *Journal of Occupational Health Psychology* 7, no. 4 (2002): 324–31.

choices, and greater agency that previous generations could only dream of. Many of us now thrive as executives, entrepreneurs, creatives, healers, and leaders, which is an empowering place to be in this world.

But while we gained new roles, we didn't always lose the old ones. Instead, we stacked them: Career woman; Caregiver; Mother; Household manager; Emotional support system. What was meant to be liberating often became overwhelming.

Yes, men's roles have expanded, too. Many contribute more at home now than in previous generations. But in my work with clients and in everyday conversations with friends, I still hear the same stories: Women who work full-time, yet carry the bulk of the housework, childcare, emotional labor, and even eldercare. And they do it quietly, often with guilt, shame, or confusion about why they're so exhausted.

I also want to include stay-at-home moms here, as they are often perceived as having "more time." In reality, their job never ends. The weekdays are packed with the demands of caregiving, errands, cleaning, cooking, and emotional regulation for everyone else. Then come the weekends—often even busier—with sports schedules, birthday parties, playdates, social coordination, and little to no downtime. It's a different kind of work, but no less demanding and draining.

This is what I call the "invisible weight," or the unspoken, unpaid, unrelenting labor that women carry in silence. It is exhausting. Part of the reason I wrote this book is so you know you're not alone, and more importantly, so you know it doesn't need to stay this way.

Why Boundaries are so Hard

If you're burned-out, chances are, your boundaries are blurred or missing altogether. This often happens when we over-function in systems that normalize women doing most of the work.

Like me, you may find yourself on autopilot—responding to every request, saying yes when you mean no—because it feels easier than disrupting the pattern. But over time, that autopilot leaves you disconnected and drained.

Burnout often comes not from one big event but from saying yes to everything and everyone . . . until the day you stop and realize there's nothing left for yourself.

That's why boundaries matter. They're not about shutting people out, but creating space for you.

The 3 Types of Boundaries

Not all boundaries are created equally. Most of us lean toward one type more than the others. Salvador Minuchin coined three types of boundaries:

- **Porous Boundaries:** Saying yes when you want to say no. Feeling guilty for setting limits. Letting others—or your job—take over your schedule and space.
- **Rigid Boundaries:** Saying no to *everything*. Withdrawing. Building walls so high that even joy and support can't get through.
- **Flexible Boundaries:** The healthy middle ground. You know when to say yes and when to say no. You protect your energy *without* shutting out the world.[3]

Reflection: Boundaries

Take a few minutes to think about your current relationship with boundaries:

- What comes to mind when you hear the word *boundaries*?

____
____
____

- Do you tend to have porous, rigid, or flexible boundaries?

____
____
____

- In which areas of your life (e.g., work, family, relationships) do boundaries feel hardest to set?

____
____
____

3 Salvador Minuchin, "Reflections on Boundaries," *American Journal of Orthopsychiatry* 52, no. 4 (1982): 655–63.

- How does the absence of boundaries affect your energy, mood, or mental health?

____

____

____

- What is one small shift you can make this week to create a healthier boundary?

____

____

____

Challenge Activity: Ask Yourself What You Need

Before we go into the three areas that can add to our burnout—time, tasks, and people—I want us to pause and ask a powerful, often overlooked question:

What do you need right now to take care of you?

This question may sound simple, but for many women, it's incredibly hard to answer because we've been conditioned to place others' needs ahead of our own. We've learned that "good" women are selfless, available, and accommodating. So, when we do start to feel burned-out, stretched thin, or resentful, we may question ourselves rather than the system we're in.

Start here:

- What do you need right now to feel more supported in your work or home life?

____

____

____

- What would help you feel less overwhelmed, more grounded, and more like yourself?

____

____

____

____

____

____

____

____

____

Now ask yourself:

- Why is it hard to ask for that?

  ____

  ____

  ____

- What fear arises if you ask for what you need?

  ____

  ____

  ____

- Now, what would you stand to gain if you asked for what you want?

  ____

  ____

  ____

I want you to start by asking someone you are close to for a small thing that would help you right now (E.g., Asking your mom to pick up the kids after school). Write down who you will ask and what you need. In CBT, this is called a **behavioral experiment.** A behavioral experiment is when you test out a worry, fear, or belief in real life. It's like a science experiment for your thoughts. Instead of just believing what your mind tells you ("If I try this, I'll fail" or "People will think I'm stupid"), make a plan to test it and see what happens. This tool is important to practice, because our thoughts often tell us negative things that aren't 100-percent true. When you test them out, you collect real evidence about what actually happens. This helps you break free from fear, avoidance, and self-doubt. Over time, your confidence will grow, and your thoughts will become more balanced and realistic. A behavioral experiment is a way to *learn by doing*, not just by thinking.

- What is the specific experiment you will try along the lines of asking someone you feel comfortable with to help you with your tasks?

  ____

  ____

  ____

- On a scale of 1–10, how uncomfortable do you feel when thinking about asking someone for support? ___________

- What do you fear will happen by asking them to help you?

  ____

  ____

  ____

- What is a possible alternative outcome?

  ____

  ____

  ____

- Now take that chance and ask the person. Write their response below:

  ____

  ____

  ____

- How uncomfortable did you feel (on a scale of 1-10) when you asked them?

  ____

  ____

  ____

- What was the outcome? Was it a response that you expected?

  ____

  ____

  ____

- What did you learn about yourself by doing this exercise?

  ____

  ____

  ____

You may worry that asking for what you need will make others perceive you as "too much," "too "difficult," or "too high-maintenance." Maybe you fear the response will be dismissed, rejected, or that nothing will change. These fears are real, but they don't need to rule you. These are fears and not facts. You are worthy of help, rest, time, and joy because you are human and you need things. You are allowed to ask. And you are allowed to set boundaries that protect your well-being.

Time Boundaries

What Time Boundaries Really Mean

Let's start with one of the most common burnout triggers, especially with work: Time boundaries.

Let's be real: The pandemic put us on a fast track to blurring our boundaries between the start and end of the workday. Sadly, Microsoft's Work Trend Index Special Report 2025 has shown that the rise of remote work has created workdays that many people cannot disconnect from, with the report calling it the "infinite workday."The data they accumulated showed that many people are unable to break free from their work.[4] This is the reality of our working world today.

Answer these questions honestly:

- Do you check your email late at night?
- Have you written an email at 10:00 p.m. and scheduled it to send at 8:00 a.m. to make it *look* like you're managing work–life balance (even when you're not)?
- Do you scroll through Teams or Slack before getting out of bed in the morning?
- Do you work weekends, even when you're exhausted?
- Do you work because you believe you can't take a break?

4 Microsoft, "Breaking Down the Infinite Workday," Work Trend Index Special Report, June 17, 2025. https://www.microsoft.com/en-us/worklab/work-trend-index/breaking-down-infinite-workday.

If you answered yes to any of these, you're not alone. But chronic availability is a quick path to burnout.

If you say it's not possible to have clear boundaries with work, I get it. Some work cultures expect employees to be ultra-available due to their customers or teams being in different time zones. Some industries require customers to have access to employees outside of traditional working hours. In some of these roles, flexibility is necessary. But if your mental health is suffering because you can't shut work off, even briefly, it's time to ask yourself if this is a sustainable long-term plan for you.

What Time Boundaries Look Like

Some things to ask yourself are:

What would it be like to . . .

- Not check work messages after 6:00 p.m.?
- Take a real lunch break, not one spent eating at my desk and looking at my computer screen?
- Say no to a meeting that could have been an email?

These are some examples of what boundaries look like.

This type of self-care fuels you for the long duration of life. These are ways to protect your focus, energy, and clarity.

My Story

I used to check emails, take work calls, and respond to texts seven days a week. The idea of unplugging from my inbox made me anxious. But I convinced myself I had to because maybe there was an emergency I needed to attend to. So, I ran a small behavioral experiment: I stopped checking emails on Sundays. The plan was to track if anything urgent came up. Week after week, month after month, I collected that data and learned that nothing catastrophic happened. If something was truly urgent, people had the necessary ways to contact me through a phone call.

The results

One small shift, just one day of disconnection, and I discovered a huge difference in my clarity, energy, and sense of control.

Reflection: Honoring Your Time

Let's take a moment to reflect on your current patterns. Write down your response to these questions:

- What time-related boundary can you set to reclaim energy? (E.g., No emails after 8:00 p.m., phone off from 9:00 p.m. to 7:00 a.m., no work on Sundays.)

  ____

  ____

  ____

- Why would this boundary be helpful to your well-being?

  ____

  ____

  ____

- What would you gain by setting this boundary?

  ____

  ____

  ____

A Hidden Burnout Culprit: Social Media

Let's talk about doomscrolling.

You know the pattern. You pick up your phone *just to check something*, and suddenly, an hour has disappeared. Or you wake up and instantly dive into social media, bombarding your brain with information before your feet even hit the floor. Trust me, I have been there. It feels like a harmless habit. But it isn't.

Late-night scrolling disrupts your circadian rhythm, your body's natural sleep–wake cycle. That throws off your sleep, increases stress, and contributes to long-term fatigue. And the more exhausted you are, the harder it becomes to set boundaries anywhere else in your life.

If you have been waking up tired, struggling to focus, or feeling constantly on edge, ask yourself:

- Am I giving my brain time to unplug from screens?
- Am I consuming content that energizes me or exhausts me?
- Do I reach for my phone when I should be sleeping, resting, or connecting?

Even small changes that include boundaries with your phones, like setting phone-free hours, turning off notifications, or keeping your phone out of the bedroom, can help your brain reset. Over time, these tiny habits can create a major shift in your energy and clarity.

Challenge Activity: Reclaim Your Time

Let's make this practical. Choose *one* area this week where you'll set a new boundary:

- Shut off work notifications at ___ p.m.
- Take a real, screen-free lunch break.
- Unplug from social media one hour before bed.
- Other:______________________________

Make a commitment to yourself. Then, each day that you set a boundary in the week, reflect on the following:

- How did you feel afterward?

  ____

- Was it uncomfortable or liberating?

  ____

- Did you feel more rested or present?

  ____

Boundaries are not about perfection. They're about small shifts that, when consistently practiced, allow you to live more intentionally. Micro-shifts can lead to big results!

Task Boundaries

What Drains You?

When we talk about burnout, we usually focus on our time or emotional load, but we often lose sight of the tasks we do every day.

Whether it's replying to emails, cleaning the kitchen, or managing everyone's schedules, many of us take on tasks by default, without questioning whether they're sustainable. Over time, those small, energy-draining responsibilities pile up, compounding stress and fatigue.

Reflection: What Drains You?

Let's take some time to pause and think about which tasks drain you and whether anything can change. Consider the following steps. Take time to think through the questions and mindfully journal your responses.

Step 1: Identify Your Level of Drain

List out your common work and home tasks.

Example:

- **Work:** responding to emails, weekly reporting, daily meetings
- **Home:** grocery shopping, bedtime routines, cooking

- Work tasks:

  ____

- Home Tasks

  ____

Then rate each one, from 0 to 100 percent, based on how much you dread doing it.

Here is a range to help you assign your level of drain:

0% Drain (Fully Energized)

- I feel completely refreshed and focused.

25% Drain (Lightly Tiring)

- I notice some effort, but it's manageable.

50% Drain (Moderately Draining)

- This task feels like work. I notice a dip in energy or motivation while doing it.

75% Drain (Highly Draining)

- I feel mentally, emotionally, or physically taxed while doing this task.

100% Drain (Completely Depleting)

- This task leaves me exhausted, overwhelmed, or burned-out.

Example:

Task: Attending a Child's School Event

- **0% Drain:** "I look forward to going, enjoy being there, and leave feeling connected."
- **25% Drain:** "It's nice, but I'm tired afterward and need a little downtime."
- **50% Drain:** "I go because I 'should,' but I feel mentally checked out and drained afterward."
- **75% Drain:** "I dread going and feel resentful about having to be there. I come home exhausted."
- **100% Drain:** "I skip the event, or go but feel numb, tearful, or completely wiped out for the rest of the day."

Now try this exercise. Assign a drain level to both your work and home tasks.

Work Tasks

Task	Drain (%)
	______%
	______%
	______%
	______%

Home Tasks

Task	Drain (%)
	______%
	______%
	______%
	______%

Now take a look. Which tasks score 70 percent or higher?

____

____

____

These likely have the biggest impact on your burnout.

Step 2: Reflect on the Impact

How do these tasks affect your energy and mood?

____

____

____

How do they spill into other parts of your life, like your sleep, relationships, or mental focus?

____

____

____

Can any of these tasks be delegated, outsourced, or restructured?

____

____

____

If you're feeling resistance about delegation, ask yourself:

- What do I fear will happen if I give this up?

  ____

  ____

  ____

- What might I gain by letting it go?

  ____

  ____

  ____

If delegation is possible:

- Is there a coworker, manager, or team member you can speak to about shifting tasks?

  ____

  ____

  ____

- Is there a family member or friend who can help lighten the load at home?

  ____

  ____

  ____

- If it's financially feasible, could you outsource things like cleaning, grocery delivery, or errands?

If delegation is not an option:

- Can you change when you do the task? (Try scheduling harder tasks for when you have the most energy.)

- Can you bundle it with something enjoyable? (E.g., Fold laundry while watching your favorite show.)

- Can you build in a small reward afterward, like a coffee or a short walk?

- What's one way you can make an energy-draining task feel easier?

Step 3: Commit to the Delegation Experiment

It is time to challenge yourself and implement some task boundaries. If letting go of control feels scary (and I understand that!), we'll start small and see what happens.

Challenge Activity: Delegation Experiment

Choose one low-risk task—at work or at home—and delegate it. Then reflect on how it went.

- Task I will delegate: ____________________
- Who will I ask to do it: ____________________
- What are my fears or negative thoughts about this?

  ____

  ____

  ____
- How much do I believe these fears to be true? (0–100%)

  ____

  ____

  ____
- What's an alternative, more balanced thought?

  ____

  ____

  ____
- How much do I believe this alternative thought? (0–100%) ____________

Reflection: After the Delegation

Capture your responses from this experience.

- Did your worst-case fears come true? Yes / No
- What actually happened?

  ____

  ____

  ____

- How did you feel? Relieved, guilty, free, worried, or a mix?

____

____

____

- What did you learn about letting go?

____

____

____

Delegation isn't just about convenience; It's about preserving your well-being. Taking care of yourself benefits you and others, because you can't fully show up for others when you're running on empty.

People Boundaries

Protecting Your Energy

Are you the one in the crowd, hand raised, saying yes to everyone, yet running on the reserve tank inside?

Constantly showing up for others—whether they're coworkers, friends, or family—without checking in with yourself first is a fast track to burnout. When your energy is already running low, it's essential to be intentional about who you give it to.

Some people leave you feeling supported and seen. Others may leave you drained, anxious, or emotionally off-balance. Perhaps you've been moving so fast you haven't even stopped to think:

- "How do I feel after I spend time with certain people?"
- "Am I walking away lighter, or am I feeling small, tired, or exhausted?"

You can even walk away feeling neutral. The key is to start noticing. And it's time to take an inventory.

Reflection: Who's in Your Circle?

Think about the people you spend time with. Ask yourself these questions and journal your responses:

- What do I enjoy most about the people I surround myself with?

  ____

  ____

  ____

- What makes it hard for me to decline social invites, even when I'm exhausted? *(Examples: fear of hurting feelings, fear of being alone, feeling obligated.)*

  ____

  ____

  ____

- Who makes me feel lighter and happier after spending time with them?

  1. ______________________
  2. ______________________
  3. ______________________

- Who do I feel drained by after spending time with them?

  1. ______________________
  2. ______________________
  3. ______________________

- Who rains on my parade when I have good news?

  ____

  ____

  ____

- Who holds space and celebrates my wins with me?

____

____

____

Now imagine that a close friend came to you feeling burned-out and anxious, saying they didn't have the energy to spend time with someone but felt obligated to do so.

As a loving friend, what would you tell them?

Now give that same advice to yourself.

____

____

____

Dig Deeper: Where Do Boundaries Feel Most Challenging?

As you reflect on the people in your life, take it one step further:

- In what situations do you struggle most to set boundaries?

____

____

____

- Are there particular people, roles, or dynamics that make it harder?

____

____

____

- What emotional or situational triggers lead you to overextending yourself?

____

____

____

Recognizing your personal boundary "blind spots" can help you plan ahead and respond more intentionally when those moments arise.

Additional Tools for Protecting Your Energy

Does your calendar feel like it belongs to everyone but you? If you're constantly overcommitting yourself, here are a few tools to help you formulate the calendar you want.

The One-In, One-Out Rule

For every yes, say one no. If you commit to a social event or extra task, ask yourself, "What can I let go of to stay balanced?"

The Delay Tactic

If your default is to say yes in the moment but regret it later, try this instead:

- "Let me think about it and get back to you."

This pause gives you time to check in with yourself:

- Do I actually want to do this?
- Do I have the capacity for this right now?

> **Personal Note:** *I use this regularly. So often, I'd ride someone else's wave of excitement and say yes, only to later think, "Why did I agree to that?" Waiting twenty-four hours has saved me countless hours and restored energy for myself. It's one of the best gifts I've given myself, thanks to a professional consultant who taught me this tool.*

Challenge Activity: The Seven-Day Energy Audit

This week, practice using the delay tactic before saying yes to any new commitment.

Each day, reflect:

- Who did I use "Let me get back to you" with?
- How did it feel to pause before responding?
- What did I notice about my own energy and decision-making?
- Would I use this approach again? Why or why not?

Self-Disclosure: Expressing Your Intentions

Setting boundaries doesn't mean being cold or avoidant. You can share your intentions with compassion and honesty. Try saying:

- "I'm trying to be more intentional with my time, so let me get back to you before agreeing."
- "I've been feeling stretched thin lately, so I can't commit to this event."

You don't owe anyone an explanation, but simple phrases like these can build understanding and even inspire others to set their own boundaries.

Additional Tip: Communicating Needs Clearly

You've spent years, or maybe even decades, holding space for others. Now it's time to hold space for yourself.

One effective tool is the "I feel" statement, which reduces defensiveness and keeps the focus on your needs, especially if the particular person drains your energy.

Instead of: "You never help with anything."

Try: "I feel overwhelmed when I manage things on my own. I need more support from you during the evenings."

That small shift opens the door to sharing your feelings and holding your boundaries in a grounded and respectful way, instead of ignoring and reacting to your environment and the people around you.

Guidelines for "I Feel" Statements:

- Use "I feel" + specific emotion + specific need.

  E.g., "I feel stretched thin when I work all day and then handle all the evening tasks. I'd love to find a new routine that works better for both of us."

- Be clear, not vague.

  Instead of: "I wish you helped more."

  Try: "Can we make a plan for you to take over bedtime three nights a week?"

- Know what's flexible and what's nonnegotiable.

  E.g., "I'm okay adjusting some things, but I need at least two hours of uninterrupted time on the weekend to recharge."

- Stay connected to your "why."

  E.g., "I want to feel more balanced and present, not resentful or depleted."

Challenge Activity: Reframe Your Statement

Think about one need and one boundary you want to communicate using the tools you just learned.

Original Statement:

(Write what you might typically say.)

____

____

____

New boundary statement with tools:

(Reframe with clarity, compassion, an "I feel" statement, and your "why" to your boundary.)

____

____

____

- What part is flexible?

  ____

- What part is non-negotiable?

  ____

- What's your deeper why?

  ____

By practicing this new way of communicating your needs and limits, you create a healthier relationship with yourself and with others. You also begin to show up differently by asking for the space and rest you need in order to thrive.

Your needs matter just as much as those of your family, coworkers, or friends. The more you show up with clarity and intention, the more others will understand, and respect, where you're coming from.

Chapter Action Items

- ☐ Consider your current relationships by answering the questions in **Reflection: Boundaries.**
- ☐ Complete the **Challenge Activity: Ask Yourself What You Need.**

Time Boundaries

- ☐ Reflect on your current patterns through **Reflection: Honoring Your Time.**
- ☐ Complete the **Challenge Activity: Reclaim Your Time.**

Task Boundaries

- ☐ Pause to consider the **Reflection: What Drains You?**
- ☐ Complete the **Challenge Activity: Delegation Experiment.**
- ☐ Capture your responses in **Reflection: After the Delegation.**

People Boundaries

- ☐ Answer the questions found in **Reflection: Who's In Your Circle?**
- ☐ Complete the **Challenge Activity: The Seven-Day Energy Audit.**
- ☐ Complete the **Challenge Activity: Reframe Your Statement.**

FINAL THOUGHTS

Boundaries are not about being the only person on the island. They're about creating the conditions for you to show up fully, authentically, and sustainably. Whether with your time, tasks, or relationships, boundaries help you reclaim your energy and direct it where it matters most.

Remember, every "no" to what drains you is a "yes" to what nourishes you. The small, consistent shifts you practice here will ripple outward, protecting your well-being and giving you the space to thrive.

CHAPTER 8

Redefining Self-Care

ALLY'S STORY

Ally woke up at 5:30 a.m., showered, got her kids ready for school, and rushed out the door with no time to eat her breakfast. She managed to drop off her kids just before the bell rang, then worked at the office until it was time to pick up her kids at 2:30 p.m.

Back at home, she juggled remote work with multiple family interruptions while also tidying up the house in between moments. Once her husband got home from work he made dinner, but after eating Ally went right back into homework duty and bedtime routines with the kids.

Finally, it was her "me" time. She grabbed a chocolate bar, promising herself she'd only have one piece, but ended up eating the whole thing. She told herself she'd watch one hour of Netflix, but four hours later, it was 1:00 a.m. She turned off the TV, frustrated with herself, already dreading the 5:30 alarm.

The next morning felt no different: exhausted, depleted, and stuck.

Ally knew it was time for a change. She decided to start her day with a five-minute meditation and a glass of warm water. She knew it wouldn't solve everything, but maybe this tiny shift would help her feel better at the start of her day. The nighttime routine still felt tricky to tackle, but for now, working on her morning routine made Ally feel like she was taking a necessary step toward reclaiming her energy.

Why This Isn't Self-Care

Sound familiar? Maybe you've been there too: numbly eating food, watching TV, or scrolling on your phone and calling it "self-care." The truth is, these habits often leave us feeling worse, not better.

I've been there myself. What looks like self-care can actually be self-sabotage—quick fixes that drain rather than restore. So, what really is self-care?

What Real Self-Care Looks Like

True self-care fills you up, nourishes your mind and body, and reconnects you to yourself. Think of it like charging your phone. If you want a fully charged battery, you let the phone rest undisturbed. But when we try to "charge" ourselves, we often slip into habits that actually serve as distractions. We don't recharge in the most helpful ways, and these distractions may even leave us more depleted.

When we are in the midst of burnout, we may feel a cognitive fog or a disconnection with life. We may seek a quick fix like a Netflix binge, eating foods that don't nourish us, drinking alcohol, using substances that modify our behavior, or going on a Target or Amazon spending spree. The issue with these behaviors is they are not actually replenishing us. These unhelpful quick fixes deplete us more than nourish us because we aren't addressing the real needs.

So, how do we change this?

Through self-reflection.

If you notice that you feel bad even when you wake up the next morning, consider what might be causing this feeling. Then, if you keep doing what you are doing, you can expect to continue to feel that same way.

But if you stop to think, "How is this behavior helping or hurting my energy? How can I feel more energized in the mornings?" This will lead you to think about what you want to change. This intentional pause to ask yourself these questions, while being honest with yourself, will start the process toward true self care.

Self care is not about numbing yourself; it is about being present in whatever you are doing. True self care is about fully recharging your battery, or filling the fuel tank of your soul.

So, what recharges you?

If you are having a hard time thinking of things, that's totally okay, because maybe this is a new way of thinking for you!

Some examples might include:

- Going on a five-minute walk outside and observing nature with no distractions.
- Reading a book.
- Calling a friend to see how they are doing.
- Taking a bath.
- Playing with your kids or pets.
- Drinking water.
- Gardening.

Reflection: What Recharges You

Capture some of your ideas of what recharges you.

Has your definition of self-care changed after reading this? If so, write down how your perspective has shifted.

Challenge Activity: Self-Care

If you haven't already, it's time to acknowledge that burnout doesn't just disappear on its own. To break free of this exhaustion cycle, you need intentional practices that restore you. If you wait until you feel motivated to practice self-care, it might never happen. Instead, create small, simple, and restorative practices that you commit to even on your most tiring days.

If you want out of the burnout cycle, doing life differently is the key. Scheduling things like exercise, social support time, or quiet time is integral in changing our behavior. In the CBT world, this act of scheduling self-care into our life is called *activity scheduling* (as mentioned in Chapter 1). To take change to the next level, we have to schedule these activities (yes, get it into your calendar!) because research shows that the act of scheduling increases the motivation to complete the task. So, if we want to change our sense of burnout, we have to schedule our way out through planning quality "me time" in.

Many of us aren't used to time for ourselves. At first, this concept may feel extremely awkward because it's a new behavior. I want you to lean into the awkwardness. Tell yourself it is normal to feel this way for a short while. But keep your focus on the prize. Consider how you will feel after your scheduled time for self care!

Let's schedule a moment right now. I want you to pick any kind of self-care activity—you can make it as big or small as you want it to be. This could be something simple like sitting in the sun with tea, texting a friend you miss, or going on a short walk. Remember, this is not about numbing or taking yourself out of your current life. It is actually plugging you into the here and now—your present moment!

Write down your chosen activity:

____

Now follow these steps:

1. Schedule time for your selected activity (I recommend inserting it on your calendar.)
2. You also can share your scheduled time here: ______________
3. When the time comes, don't cancel it. Set a timer for 5 minutes.

4. Do the activity. Fully engaging, without multitasking.
5. Then complete the Reflection: Post Self-Care Pause questions.

Reflection: Post Self-Care Pause

- How did you feel afterward? Energized? Calm? Centered?

___

___

___

- Did any unexpected emotions surface?

___

___

___

- What would it mean for you to continue prioritizing this activity?

___

___

___

- How can you realistically make time for this in your daily life?

___

___

___

Setting the Tone for Your Day

There's a saying I once heard that stuck with me: *Be a thermostat, not a thermometer.*

A thermometer reacts to its environment. A thermostat sets the tone.

When I was recovering from burnout, I realized I had been living like a thermometer. I'd wake up to immediately grab my phone to check emails, texts, and social media—before I even said good morning to myself. That screen dictated my mood! Then I would react to things that I couldn't control. For example, I would get irritated if I got a phone call at 9:00 p.m. or a text message at 1:00 a.m. These things would send me into a tailspin of thoughts like, "Who thinks it is ok to contact me at this hour? "What is wrong with them?" And when I chose to respond back, I would feel so resentful because I did it for them, not for me.

To be fair, when the obligations lessened and I had more space to think about my life, the light bulb went on and I thought, "This is not about them, this is about me!" People can do what they want, and I can choose to text back or pick up the phone when it works for me! This was a major game changer. This perspective liberated me.

I started leaving my phone in the kitchen at night, an hour before bed. At first, it felt weird and very quiet. I had muted so much noise. Over time, I started journaling again. I read more. I fell asleep more peacefully. From there, I began to untether even more from my phone. Little moments away had huge energetic impacts on me. Grocery shopping without my phone was freeing. There were less distractions, less noise, and I was getting things done faster. Soon I turned "not looking at my phone" into a game. I would see how long I could go without glancing at it. I found my mind clearer and less cluttered. This change surprised me. I loved how I felt when I needed to get things done and my phone no longer kept interrupting me.

I continued to alter my life. Instead of emails or social media in the morning, I swapped these for:

- A short YouTube meditation (10-20 minutes).
- Drinking a glass of warm water before my morning coffee.
- Journal for as long as I wanted.
- Moving my body—either by walking or hitting the gym.

By the time I checked my phone, I had already set the tone for my day, and I felt like a new person! I was no longer reacting to my environment—I was choosing and having agency over my life, and that was freeing to me.

Now I control my phone rather than it controlling me.

What about you? Can you relate to this? Do you dictate the set-up for your day or does technology, or other distractions, control the start of your day?

Reflection: Setting Your Temperature

Ask yourself:

- What would it look like if you set the tone for your day?

  ____

  ____

  ____

- What do you want to change for you to set your "temperature?"

  ____

  ____

  ____

- Describe your ideal morning ritual. What does "setting your temperature" look like?

  ____

  ____

  ____

I encourage you to try it, even if it is just for 10 minutes. You might be surprised by how powerful even just 5-10 intentional minutes of a morning ritual can shift the energy for your entire day.

If this all feels awkward or foreign, that's normal. You are doing something new, and that takes courage. At first, taking time for yourself will probably feel strange, especially if you need to implement coping strategies like asking for help, delegating tasks, or letting a few things go undone. But remember why you are doing this: to recover from your burnout. By adding these coping strategies so you can take time for self care, you are returning to your life stronger, clearer, and more connected to what matters.

Chapter Action Items

- ☐ Capture some ideas in **Reflection: What Recharges You.**
- ☐ Complete the **Challenge Activity: Self-Care.**
- ☐ Answer the questions in **Reflection: Post Self-Care Pause.**
- ☐ Identify your tone of the day through **Reflection: Setting Your Temperature.**

FINAL THOUGHTS

Without intentional self-care, we run on empty and become resentful, exhausted, and disconnected. But when we pause and commit to practices that truly nourish us, we create space for energy, clarity, and joy.

Self-care is not an indulgence. It allows us to sustain the marathon of life. It's what allows us to reset so we can respond to life rather than react to it.

I want you to claim this for yourself. Your peace, calm, and the energy to thrive is within your reach. You deserve to give yourself that gentle recharge in order to excel in this fast paced, busy world. So, take the necessary steps to show up for yourself like you do for others.

CHAPTER 9

Self-Compassion

RACHEL'S STORY

Rachel noticed the new emails flooding into her inbox and her heart pounding. It was only 9:17 a.m., and she already felt behind. Her to-do list was overflowing, and she couldn't shake the feeling that she was failing—at work, at home, at everything.

That morning, she'd snapped at her son for forgetting his lunchbox and now replayed it in her head, telling herself she was a bad mom. She beat herself up for not waking up earlier, for not being more patient, for not having it "together" like other women seemed to.

By the time her afternoon meeting started, she was exhausted. Not just from work but from the relentless inner critic telling herself she wasn't doing enough, and worse, that *she* wasn't enough.

A New Way to Speak to Yourself

Do you tend to have this biting inner voice, like Rachel, that runs wild, without letting up on your missteps or struggles? Does it leave you exhausted and just barely getting through your day? If so, this chapter is for you. In fact, this topic of self-compassion is what carried me through my own burnout and on to the other side.

For many of us, the word "self-compassion" feels unfamiliar, or even uncomfortable.

We live in a world that glorifies productivity, praises self-sacrifice, and measures worth by output. And with that comes effort coupled with self-criticism.

In some cultures, being hard on ourselves is normalized as the only way to succeed. But what if being kind to yourself was not a weakness but actually a way to thrive?

What if self-compassion could support your well-being and also help you become more creative, more present, more resilient, and yes, even more effective?

At the peak of my burnout, I functioned like a machine: Wake up, push forward, collapse into bed, repeat. I wasn't just physically drained, I was mentally brutal with myself.

My inner voice was relentless: *You're not doing enough. You're falling behind. Why can't you handle this better?*

This punishing dialogue wore me down. My anxiety was high, my self-esteem plummeted, and I couldn't even acknowledge the immense weight I carried.

What is Self-Compassion?

Dr. Kristin Neff, a pioneering researcher and scholar in self-compassion defines self-compassion with three core elements:

- **Self-Kindness vs. Self-Judgment**

  Be gentle with yourself, rather than harsh or critical when you make a mistake or fall short.

- **Common Humanity vs. Isolation**

  Recognize that suffering, failure, and imperfection are part of the human experience, not something that makes you broken or alone.

- **Mindfulness vs. Over-Identification**

  Stay aware of your thoughts and feelings without becoming overwhelmed or defined by them.

Dr. Neff's research shows that self-compassion is linked to lower anxiety, stress, and depression, as well as greater resilience, motivation, and well-being. And despite what some fear, it doesn't make you lazy or complacent. Instead, it helps you confront challenges without the crushing weight of self-judgment.[1]

Reflection: Applying Self-Compassion

Consider Dr. Neff's three-part definition:

- Have you used self-compassion before? What was it like? If you can't think of a time, what do you imagine it would feel like to practice it?

  ____

  ____

  ____

- Which of the three elements—self-kindness, common humanity, or mindfulness—feels hardest for you to practice? Why?

  ____

  ____

  ____

- Recall a recent moment of stress, failure, or burnout. How different would you have felt if you had responded to yourself with compassion rather than criticism?

  ____

  ____

  ____

Why Self-Compassion Works

Research shows that self-criticism has real consequences. Negative self-talk doesn't stay internal—it impacts how your body and mind respond.

Decades ago, psychologist Aaron Beck noted that recurring negative thoughts like "I'm not good enough" or "I always mess things up" form the foundation of depression. These thoughts shape how we interpret everyday experiences and

---

1 Kristin Neff, "What Is Self-Compassion?" *Self-Compassion Institute,* accessed October 27, 2025, https://self-compassion.org/what-is-self-compassion/.

trap us in cycles of self-blame and hopelessness.[2] More recently, researchers have found that harsh self-criticism is a major contributor to burnout. For instance, a 2022 study published in *BMC Health Services Research* found that doctors who scored high on self-critical perfectionism were more likely to experience burnout.[3]

When we constantly push ourselves while thinking we're still not doing enough, it depletes our emotional reserves. Over time, this inner pressure erodes motivation, leads to exhaustion, and distances us from the joy and meaning we once felt in our work or relationships.

This is why rediscovering self-compassion changed everything for me. It isn't about being soft or letting yourself off the hook. It's about supporting yourself when life gets hard. It's the skill of treating yourself as you would a loved one who is struggling: with kindness, patience, and encouragement. Not shame.

It's this act of love that makes all the difference!

How Would You Treat a Friend?

A powerful CBT exercise you can use as a way to restructure your thinking is to ask yourself: *If my best friend came to me with this exact struggle, what would I say to them?*

- Would you criticize them? Call them weak? Tell them to toughen up?
- Or would you comfort them, remind them of their strengths, and help them feel seen?

Now flip the script:

- Would you ever speak to a struggling friend the way you speak to yourself?
- Would you ever speak to a child the way you speak to yourself?

In my personal life, that was my gut-check moment. When I asked myself those questions, I reflected on times I lost my patience with myself—moments I wish

---

2 Aaron T. Beck, A. John Rush, Brian F. Shaw, and Gary Emery, *Cognitive Therapy of Depression* (New York: Guilford Press, 1979), 10-30.

3 S.R. Martin, "Perfectionism as a Predictor of Physician Burnout," *BMC Health Services Research* 22, no. 1 (2022): 1010, https://doi.org/10.1186/s12913-022-08785-7.

I could take back. If that's true for you, too, please know this isn't about guilt, it's about awareness.

If we strive to show grace and compassion to our family members when they fall short, don't we owe it to ourselves to do the same when we fall short?

Learning to speak to myself with kindness didn't come easily. But over time, I began to understand something important: I could become my own best friend. My own loving parent. My greatest advocate. And when I did, that's when the healing began.

The Power of Writing a Self-Compassionate Letter

One of the most transformative practices in my burnout recovery was writing letters to myself.

This isn't just journaling; it's a conscious act of kindness. It softens the inner critic and reconnects you to the part of yourself that is tired but still truly trying to do your best.

Burnout disconnected me from myself. I no longer recognized this person who kept pushing through, day after day. I kept going through the motions, but I no longer was in touch with myself. I lost my inner joy. I could be going out with a friend, or participating in a child's birthday party, but it was just a thing that I needed to cross off the "to-do" list.

Writing in a self-compassionate way helped me reconnect with myself. It reminded me that beneath all the expectations and exhaustion, I was still me—and I was worth caring for.

This became a transformational tool. It allowed me to get to know myself better, in this strange place in my life. To be with all of the feelings and thoughts I had, even those I tried to avoid behind the ongoing "to-do" list.

Challenge Activity: Write Your Self-Compassion Letter

I invite you to set aside ten to fifteen minutes to write yourself a letter. Put your phone on Airplane Mode and give yourself this time

For some, I know this may be uncomfortable, but through discomfort there may be an impact that you never knew could happen. I encourage you to try it and see how you feel after you write this letter.

Take your time. Breathe. And speak from your heart.

If you're unsure how to begin your self-compassion letter, use these prompts as a gentle guide. You don't have to answer all of the questions. Use the questions that resonate most with you. Let your answers come naturally. There are no right or wrong responses, only honesty and care.

Prompts for Your Self-Compassion Letter

- What do you want to thank yourself for? Acknowledge the strength and resilience that have brought you to where you are today.
- What feelings are you experiencing right now? Normalize them as part of the human experience.
- What obstacles have you overcome in your life? Give yourself credit for your perseverance.
- What do you need to forgive yourself for? What are you ready to release?
- How can you express gratitude for your body and all it has done for you?
- What have you learned from your triumphs and struggles?
- Moving forward, how can you be kinder to yourself in this next chapter of your life?

My Self-Compassion Letter

Reflection: The Self-Compassion Letter

After completing your letter, take a moment to pause and reflect on the experience.

- How did you feel after writing your letter? Better, worse, or neutral?

- What were some key takeaways you received from writing this letter?

- Does this tool resonate for you in your burnout journey? Why or why not?

Chapter Action Items

- ☐ Think about how you can use self-compassion in your daily life.
- ☐ Complete the **Challenge Activity: Write Your Self-Compassion Letter.**
- ☐ Pause, acknowledge how you feel, and answer the questions in **Reflection: The Self-Compassion Letter.**

FINAL THOUGHTS

It is now time to thank yourself for showing up for you. By pausing to turn inward, you've given yourself one of the greatest acts of care: self-love.

Self-love comes through self-compassion. It's not a reward that you give yourself after doing enough, but a language you use, especially when you feel the least deserving of it.

By writing a letter to yourself, you've taken a meaningful step toward healing you. You've paused the cycle of self-judgment and spoken to yourself with care. You have reminded yourself that your worth is not tied to your output or by being perfect—it is rooted in your presence, your effort, and who you are.

I hope that this way of speaking to yourself is the beginning of a new kind of relationship. One that is kind, gentle, and respectful. You've already proven your strength, and now it's time to give yourself permission to experience softness, too.

CHAPTER 10

Visualizing Your Future Self

ERICA'S STORY

Erica sat in her parked car outside the office, gripping her coffee like it was the only thing keeping her upright. The cup had gone cold ten minutes ago, but she hadn't moved. Her supervisor was on her case about deadlines again. At home, laundry was piled in the corner, the fridge was empty, and the dog hadn't been walked in two days. Every part of her felt frayed.

She couldn't remember the last time she genuinely laughed, or the last time she woke up without the weight of dread pressing on her chest. Friends kept asking if she was okay, and every time she responded that she was "just tired."

But this wasn't being tired. This was burnout.

This morning, something unexpected happened. She began to daydream about a version of herself she hadn't seen in a long time. She saw herself walking along a coastal trail, shoulders relaxed, a calm smile on her face. She wore running shoes, with her earbuds in, her dog trotting beside her. She felt energized.

The vision vanished as quickly as it came, but it opened a window of hope. Beneath the exhaustion and pressure of deadlines, a fuller version of herself still existed.

A Glimpse Beyond the Burnout

When you're in the thick of burnout like Erica, it feels like crawling through weeds, or worse, slipping deeper into quicksand. You're focused on just getting through the next hour, the next task, the next obligation. Looking ahead feels impossible because you're buried in the now.

Visualizing your future self isn't just a feel-good exercise. It's a proven technique that supports real change. In CBT, this practice is especially helpful for challenging all-or-nothing thinking, a common distortion that keeps you stuck.

When you're caught in that cycle, you believe that if you're not fully healed then you've made no progress at all. This rigid mindset ignores the slow, steady changes that actually move us forward. Visualizing your future self creates mental distance from current distress, allowing you to see that change is possible.

This practice also supports goal-setting and activity scheduling which means doing things that are healthy and meaningful, even when you don't feel like it. Because taking action can help improve your mood, when you connect with a vision of your future self, you are more likely to take intentional steps today that align with that version of you. Even small, manageable actions start to feel more meaningful because they're tied to a bigger picture.

Imagining your future self allows you to shift your focus from what's wrong right now to what's possible over time. That shift provides you with some purpose and direction during a time when you otherwise feel like you are drifting in the fog. Giving yourself permission to imagine your future gives you momentum towards what you want. It "unsticks" you from the current survival mode you are in to that future person who has healed, regained energy, and found fulfillment.

Research backs this up. Dr. Hal Hershfield at UCLA has found that when we vividly picture our future selves, we form a stronger emotional connection with them. That connection helps us act today in ways that support long-term well-being, because we're not just making choices for the exhausted version of ourselves, but also for the stronger, happier version we're becoming.[1]

This intervention was something I leaned on during my own burnout. I would imagine myself exercising at the gym, buzzing with positive energy, or walking on the beach with a pep in my step. I would also consider my feelings while

---

1 Cynthia Lee, "The Stranger Within: Connecting with Our Future Selves," *UCLA Newsroom*, April 9, 2015, https://newsroom.ucla.edu/stories/the-stranger-within-connecting-with-our-future-selves.

engaging in these activities, such as joy, peace, and a sense of reinvigoration. I focused on these feelings! This idea of the "future me" helped me take the necessary steps towards that person. When I felt stuck in survival mode, this vision pulled me forward.

Challenge Activity: Envision Your Future Self

Now it's your turn. Find a quiet place and give yourself permission to dream without limitations, fear, or guilt about your future self. Take 10–15 minutes to reflect on these questions:

- **Six months from now:** What does my life look like? What am I doing that brings energy and joy? How is it different from today?
- **Two years from now:** What does my life look like? How do I feel? Who is beside me? What supports or inspires me? If I'm still in the same career, what has shifted to make it more fulfilling?
- **Five years from now:** What parts of my life light me up? What brings me ease, meaning, and joy?

Visualization gives us a focal point that pulls us forward and reminds us that burnout doesn't need to define our life permanently.

Reflection: Your Future Self

It's time to take the vision you've created and write it down. Capture it before it fades so you can return to it again and again as a guide.

- What do you want your future self to look like?

  ____

  ____

  ____

- What habits are you cultivating now that will lead you there?

  ____

  ____

  ____

- What new habits do you need to develop?

____

____

____

This tool can help you create the distance you need from your current heavy state to a place where you dream of being. It allows you to know that you *can* create a life where you feel nourished, purposeful, and aligned to your values and goals.

Chapter Action Items

- ☐ Try the **Challenge Activity: Envision Your Future Self.**
- ☐ Answer the **Reflection: Your Future Self questions.**

FINAL THOUGHTS

Burnout can blur your vision, leaving you stuck in survival mode. But when you pause to imagine your future self, this pause guides you to the version of yourself that you want to be.

The small shifts you make today, gives you an opportunity to nurture the you that you want to be. Keep returning to that vision as a reminder that you are already on your way to burnout recovery. You are creating your future, one intentional, courageous step at a time.

CHAPTER 11

Living in Alignment with Your Values

JENNA'S STORY

Jenna stood in the middle of the aisle at the grocery store, staring at a row of salad dressings but thinking about her work projects. She couldn't remember what she came in for. Her cart had only a few scattered items: almond milk and frozen meals. The thought of making a real dinner felt impossible and exhausting.

She used to love cooking. On Sunday nights she used to blast music and try new recipes. But lately even small choices overwhelmed her. Life had become a series of checkboxes: *Finish the report, respond to the emails, schedule the dentist, don't forget your niece's birthday.*

Jenna wasn't unhappy, exactly, but she wasn't herself either. She hadn't gone hiking in months, even though nature used to ground her. She missed journaling, laughing with friends, spending quiet mornings reading. Her life looked full from the outside, but on the inside, she felt empty.

As she was deep in thought she caught herself whispering under her breath, "I don't even know what matters to me anymore."

And just like that, it clicked. Her burnout disconnected her from joy, from purpose, from her own values. Jenna had read somewhere that determining one's values can help people feel more grounded and clear about the life they want to lead. Once Jenna focused on what truly mattered to her, her life's path cleared. She realized she didn't have to do everything. She just had to start with the things that aligned with who she was.

Why Values Matter

Jenna's disconnection is a common experience that many women feel. At that moment, you wonder: "What really matters to me? What do I even stand for anymore?"

That stare Jenna had in the grocery aisle was a moment of misalignment. When we veer off track from our core values, it's easy to lose clarity, energy, and purpose.

That's why reconnecting with your values is so powerful. Values are more than preferences or ideals; they are the foundation of everything we do. They guide our decisions, shape our relationships, and influence who we are in the world. When we live in alignment with our values, life feels purposeful and clear.

This focus on values is also a core principle of **Acceptance and Commitment Therapy (ACT)**, an evidence-based therapeutic approach that blends mindfulness and behavioral-change strategies. ACT helps people live more meaningful lives by teaching them how to accept difficult thoughts and emotions, instead of avoiding them, and to take committed action that is guided by their personal values.

Rather than trying to eliminate uncomfortable feelings or control every thought, ACT encourages psychological flexibility. This model allows you to be present with what is, and to choose behaviors that align with who you truly want to be. While this book is not therapy, the idea of using your values as a compass is one of the most empowering takeaways from the ACT model. It reminds us that we can't always control our circumstances, but we can choose to live with intention based on what is important to us. When we align our lives with our values, we experience increased energy, confidence, and peace. We feel good in our body! On the other hand, when we stray from our values, and our daily actions don't reflect what matters most, we begin to feel unfulfilled, anxious, and even physically unwell.

The Cost of Misalignment

Living your values gives you a sense of direction. It reduces decision fatigue, and it makes hard choices easier because you have a clear internal guide. With each choice, you can ask: *Does this align with who I truly am?*

Imagine waking up to a life where your choices reflect what you care about most: You feel connected to your purpose. Your work feels meaningful. Your relationships thrive.

Now imagine the opposite: A life where you're constantly doing things that go against your values. You say yes because you want others to like you. You suppress your voice to avoid conflict. You chase goals that no longer inspire you. Over time, you find you always feel drained and exhausted.

For way too long, I lived in this value misalignment. I knew one of my core values is helping others, but over the years, that became my only focus—more like a hyperfocus. I was the "can-do" person, neglecting other important values like physical health, personal and professional growth, and social connection. Because I was moving away from so many of my cherished values, my body and soul felt it—a heaviness pressed against my shoulders. I didn't fully see it at the moment, but in hindsight, I realized how much I neglected myself. Only when I recentered my values did I feel lighter, clearer, and alive again.

Research backs this up. Dr. Kelly McGonigal, a health psychologist at Stanford University, found that when people live in conflict with their values, the body reacts as if it's under threat. The nervous system shifts into fight-or-flight, leading to tension, headaches, and fatigue. On the flip side, living in alignment with your values activates the brain's reward system, releasing dopamine and boosting well being.[1]

Defining Your Core Values

If you already know your values, that's wonderful! If not, we will figure it out together. Discovering, reaffirming, or reconnecting to your values will remind you of what truly matters most!

To begin, circle or highlight any values that resonate with you. Add your own if something is missing—this list is just a starting point.

---

1 Kelly McGonigal, The Upside of Stress: Why Stress Is Good for You, and How to Get Good at It (New York: Avery, 2015), 37–90.

- Helping Others
- Physical Health
- Fairness
- Travel
- Religion/Spirituality
- Career/Professional Growth
- Family
- Abundance
- Leadership
- Honesty
- Trustworthiness

Are there other values not listed that are of high importance to you? If you want to see a more extensive list of values, **Brené Brown's List of Values** is more comprehensive, with around 100 values that you can look at to build your own list.[2]

Reflection: Core Values

Now take a moment to reflect on the values you selected.

- What did you learn about yourself when you identified these values?

____

____

____

____

- How do you currently express these values in your life?

____

____

____

____

2 Brené Brown, "Dare to Lead List of Values," Brené Brown, accessed December 15, 2025, https://brenebrown.com/resources/dare-to-lead-list-of-values/.

- In what ways does your work align—or not align—with these values?

____
____
____
____

- Are there habits, relationships, or routines that conflict with what matters most to you?

____
____
____
____

- Are there values you deeply care about but haven't prioritized?

____
____
____
____

Challenge Activity: Align with Your Values

It is time to bring more alignment into your life with your values. This activity will help you put together a plan to do this.

1. Choose your top five values.

1. ____________________
2. ____________________
3. ____________________
4. ____________________
5. ____________________

2. **Now rank them on a scale of 1 to 5**
(1 = Not living it at all, 5 = Fully aligned).

Values	Rank

3. **For these values, ask yourself these questions:**

- What small steps can I take to integrate this value more into my daily life?

____
____
____
____

- What obstacles prevent me from living this value fully?

____
____
____
____

- How can I restructure my priorities to honor what matters most?

____
____
____
____

Chapter Action Items

- ☐ Identify your top five values.
- ☐ Consider how your life aligns (or doesn't) to these core values by answering the questions in **Reflection: Core Values.**
- ☐ Complete the **Challenge Activity: Align with Your Values.**

FINAL THOUGHTS

Living in alignment with your values is the foundation for a life grounded in what matters most. When burnout pulls you away from that foundation, it's often because you've moved away from your values. The distractions of people-pleasing and endless obligations can derail you, but reconnecting to your values brings you back on track.

Our values are our North Star. By following them, we return to clarity, peace, and purpose. And when we align our actions with what matters most to us, we partake in one of the most powerful medicines against burnout.

CHAPTER 12

Honoring Change and Adaptation in the Seasons of Our Lives

ELLA'S STORY

Ella used to be the kind of woman who thrived on structure. Early morning workouts, a full client load, regular dinner parties with friends, and a vision board packed with goals. Her planner was color-coded, her calendar full, and her days productive. She prided herself on being someone who showed up energized, dependable, and always moving forward.

But lately, everything felt different. Her energy was flat, and her motivation was unpredictable. She canceled more plans in the last two months than she kept. The workouts she once loved now felt like a chore. Some mornings, she didn't want to get out of bed—not from depression, exactly, but from a deep, soul-level fatigue she couldn't shake.

At first, Ella fought it. She pushed harder, told herself to "get it together," forcing productivity because that had always worked before. But instead of snapping out of it, she burned out more. She was living by the same rules she had set during a completely different season of her life.

One afternoon, she sat with a blank journal page and wrote at the top: *What season am I in?*

The words poured out. She realized she was in a season of letting go: a quieter season that needed stillness, gentleness, and more space. Not forever, but for now. Her values hadn't changed—health, connection, growth—but how she honored them needed to.

That shift didn't mean she was failing. It meant she was adapting. Healing. Listening.

Why Seasons Matter

As you begin to heal, you may notice that your values no longer fit the ways you once lived. This means you're entering a new season, and your values are ready to be expressed differently.

Understanding your values is powerful, but it's just as important to recognize that how you live them will shift depending on the season of life you're in. Some seasons make it easy to live fully aligned with your values. Other seasons require flexibility, patience, and grace.

For example, after my parents passed, everything about my life shifted. Exercise had always grounded me. I tried to keep up the same workout routine, pushing myself to maintain it like I always had. However, instead of feeling stronger after workouts, I felt depleted. It took some time, but I eventually understood: My body wasn't asking for an intense workout; rather, it was asking for gentleness. Before, my body hungered for those huge endorphin rushes from my workouts, but I had to acknowledge and accept that I wasn't in that season of striving anymore. Instead, I was in a season of grief, burnout, healing, and restoration.

So I had to pivot. I started taking short walks outside in the sunlight among the big trees. In place of pushing through intense workouts, bright indoors lights, and booming music, I now gave myself permission to be in nature, to take walks with the sun on my face, and move my body at a slower pace. I also did more yoga.

This shift to a gentler exercise routine let something else shift inside me. I honored my value of physical well-being in a way that was *aligned* with the reality of where I was. The good news: I knew I was headed in the right direction because, compared to my former cardio-crazed gym workouts, after my walks, I actually felt more replenished and filled with energy again.

This is what it means to acknowledge the season that you are in. It's about allowing yourself to change. By not being a critic or taskmaster, I let go, and for the first time in my life, I truly became a compassionate friend to myself. I caringly told my body: *"It's okay. You're doing enough. Let's rest for a while."*

That's what it means to acknowledge your season: To let go of rigid expectations, align your life with your values, and treat yourself with compassion.

Reflection: Your Life Season

Take a few quiet moments to reflect on where you are, and how you can adapt with care. Consider these questions and write down your responses.

- Is there a value you're currently pushing yourself to uphold, even though it's draining you?

  ____

  ____

  ____

- What would it look like to honor that value in a different way during your current season of life?

  ____

  ____

  ____

- What do you need to accept about this current season of your life in order to move through this phase with more ease?

  ____

  ____

  ____

- How might softening your approach to living your values bring you more peace and fulfillment?

  ____

  ____

  ____

Challenge Activity: Seasons of Your Life

Now that you've reflected on your current season, let's explore how to bring your values into this chapter of life.

- **Name Your Season:** What would you call this chapter of your life right now? (E.g., healing, transition, rebuilding, quiet joy.)

  ____

  ____

  ____

- **Describe it in Three Words:** Honest words that capture your reality. (E.g., foggy, slow, sacred.)

  ____

  ____

  ____

- **Create a Mantra or Phrase:** Something simple that feels like a hand on your heart. (E.g., "I'm allowed to rest;" "Gentle is still strong;" "I don't have to rush.")

  ____

  ____

  ____

- **Choose One Small Act:** A walk, a phone call, canceling something, setting a timer for rest, or whatever feels supportive right now.

  ____

  ____

  ____

This activity is all about honoring you and aligning your energy with what this season of life actually needs!

Chapter Action Items

- ☐ Identify your current season through **Reflection: Your Life Season.**
- ☐ Complete the **Challenge Activity: Seasons of Your Life.**

FINAL THOUGHTS

Knowing your values gives you a framework for living with purpose. But living your values with compassion, especially as life changes, is what brings peace into your life.

Keep checking in with yourself. Keep adjusting with care. Keep honoring what matters most, even if how you express it changes over time.

Your values are your guide. Honor them in the way that serves you best right now, and they will carry you forward into the life you truly desire.

CHAPTER 13

The Power of Small Wins

SAMANTHA'S STORY

Samantha was a high-performing professional who prided herself in her resilience—until she hit a wall. Suddenly, even the smallest tasks felt insurmountable. She found herself crying in the shower and mentally checking out during conversations. She believed the only way to fix her life was a total overhaul: quit her job, move somewhere new, and start from scratch. But every time she thought about making a big change, she froze, too tired and too uncertain.

One morning, instead of reaching for her phone first thing, she took a deep breath and said aloud: "Just one thing today." That "one thing" was a five-minute walk. The next day, she made her bed. She wasn't reinventing her life overnight, but she was rebuilding her sense of agency one small win at a time.

The Big vs. the Small

Can you relate to Samantha? Maybe you're in a season where everything feels like too much. Maybe you've forgotten what it's like to celebrate the micro-victories. If so, this chapter is for you. There was a time when I believed transformation had to be big, that to move forward in my life, I had to start over and reinvent everything—burn the old version of me to the ground and rise from the ashes. But my journey through burnout taught me the opposite: real, sustainable change usually doesn't happen through radical overhauls. It happens through small, steady wins—moments where you choose differently, even when it feels insignificant. Over time, those small choices build into the foundation for recovery.

Rewiring the Burnout Brain

When we're in burnout mode, everything feels heavier. From the psychological perspective of CBT, this state often activates a mental trap called **negative filtering**. This is when your brain fixates only on what is wrong in your life and overlooks what is going right.

The more we practice negative filtering, the stronger it becomes, like a muscle we've over-trained. Over time, this pattern can lead to increased anxiety, low mood, and even feelings of hopelessness.

But the good news is we can retrain our brains. Focusing on small wins is a powerful exercise that shifts the filter toward balance. It feels awkward at first, but over time, it builds what I call a **positive filter**, or a more realistic way of viewing your day and your accomplishments. Over time, this shift boosts motivation, confidence, and a sense of control. Small wins may look minor, but they are how we recover from burnout.

Why Small Wins Matter

As women, we are faced with so many things thrown at us daily that when we do something that may be a win to us, we don't even pause to acknowledge it. We think, "Well, I should have been doing this all along" or "Other people manage this easily, so there is nothing to acknowledge here." But this way of thinking keeps us stuck in burnout.

Small wins matter because they:

- Build momentum and motivation.
- Change the internal narrative from "I can't" or "I don't" to "I can" or "I did."
- Prove to yourself that progress is happening, even in survival mode.

Research backs this up. Harvard professors Teresa Amabile and Steven Kramer found that even small steps forward in meaningful work significantly boost motivation and engagement. They called this the Progress Principle: That real change builds from small and consistent steps, not grand gestures.[1]

---

1 Teresa M. Amabile and Steven J. Kramer, *The Progress Principle: Using Small Wins to Ignite Joy, Engagement, and Creativity at Work* (Boston: Harvard Business Review Press, 2011), 80-110.

Celebrating the Small Wins

We live in a world that celebrates the big stuff: promotions, transformations, new relationships, and major achievements. Yes, those are moments we want to honor. However, it is equally important to give credit for every small decision we make along the way.

Learning to celebrate small wins means redefining what those wins are. It's about giving yourselves credit for the choices you make that align with your well-being, even if no one else notices.

Small wins that honor you might look like any of these examples:

- Drinking a glass of water before coffee in the morning.
- Turning off your phone ten minutes before bed.
- Saying no to something that drains your energy.
- Taking a deep breath before reacting in frustration.
- Eating lunch away from your desk, without screens.
- Writing one sentence in your journal, even if it's just: "I'm here."

Each time you follow through on a small, positive behavior, your brain rewards you with a burst of dopamine. This feel-good chemical boosts our confidence and motivation, encouraging us to repeat the behavior. It's a physiological reason to celebrate every small win.

My Story of Small Wins

When I stepped down from my role as clinical director, I was so exhausted I often stayed in bed until late morning, responding to emails and scrolling on my phone. As a therapist, I knew what I "should" do, but I couldn't bring myself to do it. However, this also gave me compassion and empathy for my clients who were struggling with making a change for themselves. With patience, I worked on getting out of bed, earlier and earlier, while focusing on these little wins. This led me to where I am now: Realizing that I feel so much better when I get out of bed first thing in the morning. Without acknowledging the small wins, I know my life would be very different today. We have to celebrate our behavior changes, and these celebrations of micro-changes lead us to the macro-shifts in our lives!

Reflection: Noticing Your Small Wins

Now that we know the powerful research about filtering and focusing on the small wins, let's take a moment to reflect on building our small-wins muscle.

To help you reflect on your small wins, consider these questions:

1. What small win, no matter how minor, can you acknowledge from today or this week? (E.g., I got out of bed on a hard day, I responded to an email I was avoiding, I asked for help.)

   ____
   ____
   ____

2. When you think back on your week, what moments of effort, progress, or resilience did you overlook because you were focused on what went wrong?

   ____
   ____
   ____

3. What specific action can you commit to over the next seven days to build your "positive filter" muscle? (**Tip:** Start a small wins journal or simply jot one win per day on your calendar.)

   ____
   ____
   ____

4. Can you think of a small win in your past that eventually led to a bigger transformation?

   ____
   ____
   ____

5. How can you intentionally celebrate your small wins moving forward?

   ____
   ____
   ____

Challenge Activity: Celebrate the Small Wins

Now that you have an idea of how much the small-wins-lens shows up in your life, I want you to practice this skill over the next seven days. Write down one win you accomplished each day. If you need ideas, revisit the list of small wins reviewed earlier.

Monday Small Win: ______________________________

Tuesday Small Win: ______________________________

Wednesday Small Win: ______________________________

Thursday Small Win: ______________________________

Friday Small Win: ______________________________

Saturday Small Win: ______________________________

Sunday Small Win: ______________________________

Remember, the more we focus on the good we've done, the more we create a positive filter in our brain. This awareness of the good provides momentum, moving us closer to the life we want to live.

Chapter Action Items

- ☐ Consider the questions in **Reflection: Noticing Your Small Wins.**
- ☐ Complete the **Challenge Activity: Celebrate the Small Wins.**

FINAL THOUGHTS

You don't have to make a massive overhaul in your life to create meaningful change. Some of the most meaningful shifts in your life will come from focusing on even our smallest wins. Small wins are powerful because, as research shows us, it leads to feeling more motivated to continue the behavior, which leads to greater change.

Keep returning to the present and ask yourself, "What's one small thing I can do today that honors me?" Then do that.

And when you do, pause long enough to notice it. Taking this moment to acknowledge that you did something good for yourself rewires your brain, builds your trust and agency, and reinforces that you're capable of progress in the middle of burnout, one small win at a time. And as you focus on those small wins, they will build upon themselves, leading you to a life beyond burnout.

CHAPTER 14

Reintegrating into Life after Burnout

LAURA'S STORY

Laura sat in her car outside the office building. It had been five months since she'd left on medical leave for burnout. Five months of unlearning the pace that nearly broke her. She had meditated, gone to therapy, journaled through the tears, and slept—*really* slept—for the first time in years.

Now she was "better." At least, better enough to return to work.

However, she wasn't sure if she would lose herself in work again. Would she slip back into people-pleasing and perfectionism, chasing achievement like a drug?

What scared her more than relapsing into burnout was the fear that everything she'd learned might not stick.

So, before stepping out of her car, she took a deep breath and told herself: *I won't go back to the version of me that broke. I'm coming back differently now.*

Moving Into A New Normal

Have you ever felt like Laura? Feeling healed enough to move forth in the world, but the world expects you to return exactly as you were—faster, busier, and always "on"?

Coming back to life after burnout isn't as simple as flipping a switch. The world keeps moving, responsibilities still exist, and the pull to fall back into old patterns is strong. But the reality is that you are not the same. Experiencing burnout forces a pause, and now, as you begin to reengage with life, your goal is to return in a way that protects what you've learned.

When I was finally ready to return to work, I was terrified and anxious. Would I slip back into old patterns? Would I say yes too often? Would I once again trade my well-being for people-pleasing and hyperproductivity?

The fear was real, but so was my determination. I didn't want to lose what I'd found, and I didn't want to give up on the quality of life I had created for myself. So I made a promise to myself: I would build a life that honors my energy, aligns with my values, and celebrates small wins.

My professional consultant and I worked on keeping my word to the work schedule that served me best. No more saying yes to clients at 8:00 p.m. because that compromised my evening routine sleep. No more saying yes in the moment just to please others. Of course, I had some slipups (and I still do at times). But that's what reintegration looks like. It isn't perfection but *intention*—the intention to carry forward what you've learned, say yes only when it aligns with your values, rest daily before it becomes urgent, and let small wins be enough.

Because our behaviors are so ingrained, reflexive, and automatic, I want you to think through the questions below so you can show up to your professional self as "You 2.0."

A Framework for Sustainable Recovery

Coming back to life after burnout is less about "bouncing back" and more about creating daily routines that support you, without falling into the same patterns that once drained you. Many people talk about bouncing back after burnout, which reflects resilience as you return to where you were before. But resilience alone isn't the full picture: Thriving goes a step further. Thriving means not just surviving or recovering, but growing into a healthier, more intentional version of yourself. It's carrying forward the lessons you've learned, honoring your boundaries, and creating a life that's not only sustainable, but deeply fulfilling.

The Relapse Prevention Burnout Plan offers a structured way to intentionally protect your energy, maintain balance, and build a life that supports ongoing healing and growth.

Challenge Activity: Relapse Prevention Burnout Plan

This is your opportunity to become crystal clear on what matters most and what you refuse to sacrifice again.

Ask yourself:

What are your top three priorities for your well-being?

1. ______________________________
2. ______________________________
3. ______________________________

What boundaries will you set around work, relationships, and personal time?

____

____

____

What is one thing you absolutely will not compromise on again?

____

____

____

These nonnegotiables are your foundation. They are your anchors moving forward.

Reflection: Create a Sustainable Routine

You don't need a "perfect" schedule. You need a sustainable rhythm—one that includes rest, joy, movement, and meaningful work, not just busyness and productivity.

Reflect on:

- What does an ideal, balanced day look like for you?

  ____
  ____
  ____

- How can you build in rest *before* you need it?

  ____
  ____
  ____

- What small, grounding habits can anchor your day?

  ____
  ____
  ____

- Do you have agency over what your days look like?

  - What small steps can I take to integrate this value more into my daily life?

    ____
    ____
    ____

  - What obstacles prevent me from living this value fully?

    ____
    ____
    ____

Warning Signals and Triggers of Burnout

As you return to your busy work- and home-life responsibilities with new thoughts and behaviors, it's important to be aware of early warning signals of a potential burnout relapse.

These signals are different from one person to the next, so it's important you know what to look for in your own life. Then, by recognizing the signs, you can decide how to take care of yourself to pivot back into a state of balance.

Warning signals might include:

- Feeling more irritable or impatient than usual.
- Increased brain fog, forgetfulness, or difficulty focusing.
- Dreading work or procrastinating on tasks you normally handle well.
- Skipping meals or reaching for quick, unhealthy food instead of nourishing options.
- Noticeable loss of motivation or enthusiasm for your work or personal life.
- Trouble sleeping, or waking up unrefreshed.
- Withdrawing from social connections or avoiding activities you normally enjoy.
- Feeling tense in your body (tight shoulders, headaches, fatigue).

Be mindful of your triggers to burnout as well. These can include:

- Taking on extra commitments without rest.
- Working past your scheduled end time or checking emails after hours.
- Lack of sleep or poor rest.
- Skipping exercise or movement routines that help you recharge.
- Neglecting hobbies or time with loved ones to complete work.
- Unclear boundaries with colleagues or family.
- High-stress deadlines without recovery time afterward.

Reflection: Identify Warning Signals and Personal Triggers

From these lists, or from your own awareness, list out your warning signals and personal triggers.

My warning signals are:

___

___

___

My personal triggers are:

___

___

___

If you see these behaviors creeping back up into your life, that's okay. We are human, and we can get back on track. But how do you want to handle these warnings?

Here are some ideas of how to reset yourself:

- **Quick resets:** deep breathing, journaling, a short walk.
- **Longer resets:** take a personal day, digital detox, a weekend of rest.

Support System

- Identify 2–3 people you can check in with when you notice signs of relapse (a friend, coach, therapist, or mentor).
- Share your plan with at least one person who can help hold you accountable.

Relapse Prevention

- Weekly check-in: "Am I honoring my nonnegotiables?"
- Monthly review: "How did I do with sticking to my set schedule? How did I do with taking breaks, setting boundaries, and engaging in self-care?"

Be prepared to adjust workload, commitments, or routines if burnout signs creep back in.

Be Mindful of Overcommitment

Feeling better doesn't mean it's time to overfill your calendar. Your energy is sacred now. Treat it that way.

I struggled with this. I used to say yes out of guilt, obligation, or habit because I *could*. But later, I realized I had compromised my well-being in the process. I had to learn the hard way that I could not keep overcommitting myself.

So, it's time for you to protect yourself. From all you have now learned, promise yourself not to fall into this easy trap. Before saying yes to commitments, ask yourself:

- Does this align with the life I'm creating?
- How will I check in with myself to avoid overload?
- What are my personal warning signs that I'm taking on too much?

Let discernment be your superpower.

Reflection: Shift Your Mindset

One of the trickiest traps during post-burnout is slipping back into the belief that your worth equals your output.

This was my Achilles' heel. But here's what I've learned: *You are valuable without constantly achieving. Your rest is your recharge time.*

Reflect on these questions:

- How will I remind myself that rest is productive and beneficial?
- How can I cultivate presence, not just performance?
- What outdated beliefs about productivity do I need to unlearn?

Chapter Action Items

- ☐ Define your nonnegotiables through the **Challenge Activity: Relapse Prevention Burnout Plan.**
- ☐ Consider what you want your life to look like by completing **Reflection: Create a Sustainable Routine.**
- ☐ Complete **Reflection: Identify Warning Signals and Personal Triggers.**
- ☐ Answer the questions in **Reflection: Shift Your Mindset**.

FINAL THOUGHTS

Reintegrating after burnout means living as the version of yourself who knows better now—the one who listens more deeply, chooses more intentionally, and protects peace with fierce compassion.

You are not the same person who burned out. You carry the tools to care for yourself in ways you didn't before. Intentionality is now your best friend. Stay aware of how you feel, pay attention to your self-talk, and stay true to the version of you that you know is healthiest.

Wherever your journey takes you next, remind yourself: You deserve a life that feels good to live. At the end of the day, you have the power to protect your well-being—one choice at a time.

Now go create it.

Conclusion

Burnout is not the end of your story. In many ways, it can be the beginning of a new chapter. You have learned from the heaviness and exhaustion, and now you're ready to step into a life that feels balanced, fulfilling, and completely your own.

The tools in this workbook are meant to give your mind, body, and heart what they've been craving: practical strategies, meaningful reflections, and gentle encouragement to help you shift from surviving to thriving.

I have faith in you and that you have the power to change how you live, how you work, and most importantly, how you care for yourself. Remember I, too, know the exhaustion, the self-doubt, and the heavy feeling of being stuck in an unsustainable cycle. And I've been on the other side, discovering what's also waiting for you when you recenter your life. Clarity, energy, and a renewed sense of purpose are within reach!

This journey is not about perfection; it's about progress. When you notice you're drifting back into old patterns, gently choose to return to what supports you. Every time you pause, reflect, or perform one small, intentional action, you are honoring yourself and building a life that supports who you want to become.

I believe in your capacity to create a life that supports you—not just one that looks good on the outside, but one that feels good on the inside, too. And when you need to, remember, you can reach out to a therapist, a coach, a trusted friend, or a family member along the way.

So take what you've learned here and trust that every small, intentional shift you make moves you closer to who you truly are.

You are capable of shining bright on this earth.

Your best, most thriving self is waiting. Recenter your life and go start living again!

Lisa Macedo, LMFT

Bibliography

Amabile, Teresa M., and Steven J. Kramer. *The Progress Principle: Using Small Wins to Ignite Joy, Engagement, and Creativity at Work.* Boston: Harvard Business Review Press, 2011.

American Psychological Association. s.v. "Burnout." APA Dictionary of Psychology. Last modified April 19, 2018. https://dictionary.apa.org/burnout.

Beck, Aaron T., John Rush, Brian F. Shaw, and Gary Emery. *Cognitive Therapy of Depression.* New York: The Guilford Press, 1979.

Brown, Brené. "Dare to Lead List of Values." Brené Brown. Accessed December 15, 2025. https://brenebrown.com/resources/dare-to-lead-list-of-values/.

Bybee, Jane, Rolande Mensca, and Rashid Velasco. "The Development of Reactions to Guilt-Producing Events." In *Guilt and Children*, edited by Jane Bybee, 185-213. San Diego: Academic Press, 1998.

Cloud, Henry, and John Sims Townsend. *Boundaries: When to Say Yes, How to Say No, to Take Control of Your Life.* Grand Rapids, MI: Zondervan, 1992.

Freudenberger, Herbert J. "Staff Burn-Out." *Journal of Social Issues* 30, no. 1 (1974): 159-65.

Lee, Cynthia. "The Stranger Within: Connecting with Our Future Selves." UCLA Newsroom, April 9, 2015. https://newsroom.ucla.edu/stories/the-stranger-within-connecting-with-our-future-selves

Martin, S. R. "Perfectionism as a Predictor of Physician Burnout." *BMC Health Services Research* 22, no. 1 (2022): 1010. https://doi.org/10.1186/s12913-022-08785-7.

Maslach, Christina, Susan E. Jackson, Michael P. Leiter, and Wilmar B. Schaufeli. "Individual Report: MBI-GS." Mind Garden. Accessed December 19, 2025. https://www.mindgarden.com/mbi-general-survey/177-mbigs-individual-report.html.

McGonigal, Kelly. *The Upside of Stress: Why Stress Is Good for You, and How to Get Good at It.* New York: Avery, 2016.

Microsoft. "Breaking Down the Infinite Workday." Work Trend Index Special Report. June 17, 2025. https://www.microsoft.com/en-us/worklab/work-trend-index/breaking-down-infinite-workday.

Minuchin, Salvador. "Reflections on Boundaries." *American Journal of Orthopsychiatry* 52, no. 4 (1982): 655-63.

Neff, Kristen. "What is Self-Compassion?" Self-Compassion Institute. Accessed October 27, 2025. https://self-compassion.org/what-is-self-compassion/.

Schaufeli, Wilmar B., and Dieter Enzmann. *The Burnout Companion to Study and Practice: A Critical Analysis.* London: Taylor & Francis, 2024.

Tangney, June P., Ronda L. Dearing, and Darleine L. Wagner. "Shame and Guilt in Adaptive and Maladaptive Self-Evaluations." *Journal of Occupational Health Psychology* 7, no. 4 (2002): 324-31.

Tangney, June Price, and Ronda L. Dearing. *Shame and Guilt.* New York: The Guilford Press, 2002.

The National Institute for Occupational Safety and Health. "Module 2 Outline: What burnout is and is not." CDC. Last modified March 8, 2023. https://www.cdc.gov/niosh/learning/publichealthburnoutprevention/module-2/outline.html.

Activity Resources

Chapter 2: The Signs of Burnout

Maslach Burnout Inventory (MBI – General Survey)

To access the Maslach Burnout Inventory survey:

1. Visit www.mindgarden.com
2. Select the **Search** option in the upper-right corner of the page
3. Enter *Individual Report:* MBI-GS in the search bar
4. Select **MBI: General Survey – Individual Report (MBI-GS)**
5. Choose **Add to cart** and follow the checkout instructions

Note: *The MBI is a paid assessment provided by Mind Garden, Inc. At the time of printing, the survey cost $15. Pricing and availability may change.*

Challenge Activity: Burnout Inventory

Follow-Up Questions:

- What score did you get?

____

- Did the score surprise you? Why or why not?

____

____

- Any additional thoughts about your score?

____

____

Worksheet Prompt: Burnout or Grief?

How do you know if the emptiness you feel is due to burnout or grief? Take a few minutes to answer these questions and reflect on your responses:

1. **What is the source of my exhaustion right now?**
   - Ongoing demands, overwork, or caregiving strain (Burnout)
   - Loss or major life change (Grief)
   - Both
2. **How do my emotions feel?**
   - Flat, numb, detached, irritable (Burnout)
   - Sad, longing, waves of pain or yearning (Grief)
3. **What brings me relief?**
   - Rest, boundaries, reduced workload (Burnout)
   - Talking, ritual, space to feel the loss (Grief)
4. **What do I need most right now?**
   - Energy restoration
   - Emotional support
   - Both

Chapter 3: The Nervous System and Burnout

Reflection: Body Check-In

Take a moment to gently check in with your body and mind. Consider these questions and write down your response.

- How does your body typically respond to stress or overwhelm?

  ____

  ____

  ____

- Can you recall a time when your nervous system felt stuck in "high alert"? What do you remember about how your body responded?

  ____

  ____

  ____

Chapter 4: Learning Who We Are

Challenge Activity: Monitor Your Symptoms

One of the most effective tools we can use from CBT is monitoring your symptoms. Just like you might track your spending or your workouts, you will want to track daily how often you notice the three key burnout symptoms: exhaustion, cynicism, and a sense of ineffectiveness.

The Daily Sumptom-Monitoring Sheet

Directions:

Every night, for a month, rate your three core burnout symptoms on a scale from **0–10** (0 = not present at all, 10 = at the extreme level). Then complete the reflection questions to increase your awareness of patterns.

Ratings:

- My Exhaustion level today (0–10): ________
- My Cynicism (pessimism, irritability, or loss of empathy) level today (0–10): ________
- My Ineffectiveness/Lack of Accomplishment level today (0–10): ________

If you monitor your symptoms for a month, **(use what is practical for you, the notes app of your phone, a notebook)** you will discover patterns that otherwise you might miss. These patterns will become your roadmap for change.

Reflection: Notice Your Symptoms

What did you notice today about your exhaustion, cynicism, and feelings of ineffectiveness? Write down your observations:

1. Did your **exhaustion** go up or down? What were you doing? Who were you with?

   ____

   ____

2. How about your **cynicism**? What increased or decreased it today?

   ____

   ____

3. Did you feel **ineffective** in your work or day-to-day tasks? What helped or hurt?

   ____

   ____

4. Did you learn anything new with tracking these symptoms?

   ____

   ____

5. Can you identify what might prevent these symptoms from changing?

   ____

   ____

Chapter 5: The Power of Our Beliefs

Challenge Activity: Shift a Belief

Step 1: Identify the Limiting Belief

Step 2: Challenge the Belief

Step 3: Replace with a Balanced Belief

Now you try:

What belief do you have that fuels your burnout?

____

____

____

How can you challenge and reframe this belief in a way that serves you better?

____

____

____

Reflection: Your Genetic Disposition

Consider these questions. Capture your thoughts in the lines below.

1. When you think about the emotional patterns in your family—worry, avoidance, irritability, over-responsibility, or perfectionism—what parallels do you notice in yourself today?

   ____

   ____

   ____

2. How have these inherited tendencies helped you in certain seasons of your life, and in what ways have they made things harder?

   ____

   ____

   ____

3. Knowing what you now understand about your genetic and family patterns, what is one gentle shift you'd like to make to support your well-being moving forward?

___

___

___

Reflection: Your Beliefs

Now it's your turn. Reflect on your beliefs by answering these questions:

- What messages did my family tell or model to me about work and rest?

___

___

___

- When was I praised? When was I criticized?

___

___

___

- How did that shape my beliefs about worth?

___

___

___

Work Beliefs

- Do I feel more worthy when I'm productive?

___

___

___

- What would happen if I did less but still earned the same?

___

___

___

Rest Beliefs

- Do I feel guilty when I rest? Why?

  ____
  ____
  ____

- What other emotions surface when I slow down?

  ____
  ____
  ____

Self-Worth Beliefs

- What do I believe makes a person worthy?

  ____
  ____
  ____

- What would I tell a friend who believed the same thing?

  ____
  ____
  ____

Challenge Activity: Create an Empowering Mantra

Now create your own mantra:

1. Identify a belief that no longer serves you.
2. Imagine your best friend saying it. What would you tell them?
3. Reframe it into a supportive mantra here:
    - ____________________
    - ____________________
    - ____________________

Now wear it loud! Put it on a sticky note, sing it in the shower, or repeat it before bed. At the end of the day, journal your observations. How did you feel living by this mantra?

Chapter 6: The Emotional Math of Burnout—Guilt and Shame

Reflection: Shame and Guilt

Pause to answer these questions.

1. **When have you felt guilt recently?**

How did you respond?

Did it lead to helpful action, or did it just drain you?

2. **Does shame show up in your self-talk?**

In those moments, what does your inner voice say about you?

______

______

______

How do those thoughts affect your relationships or daily life?

______

______

______

Challenge Activity: "Should" Statements

Take a moment to notice any "shoulds" you have been carrying in the back of your mind lately. Write down 3–5 of them below.

______

______

______

______

______

______

Then ask yourself:

- Whose voice is this really? Is it mine, or does it come from a parent, teacher, society, or an old belief?

  ______

  ______

  ______

- Is this "should" statement helpful or harmful? Does it motivate me, or does it leave me feeling ashamed or inadequate?

  ______

  ______

  ______

- What can I say instead? Reframe the statement with kindness and truth.

  E.g., Replace "I should be more productive" with "I'm doing my best, and rest is productive, too."

  ____

  ____

  ____

Remember, awareness is the first step to breaking free from guilt and shame.

Challenge Activity: Write and Balance a Guilt/Shame-Based Thought

Now you try. Pick one thought that makes you feel guilt or shame:

Step 1: Record this negative thought.

Step 2: Examine and record the evidence that supports this thought.

Step 3: Examine and record the evidence that goes against this thought.

Step 4: Based on the evidence of both sides from above, what is a more balanced thought you can write, that you believe blends the two sides?

Negative Thought:	
Evidence For:	**Evidence Against:**
Balanced Thought:	

Chapter 7: Boundaries—The Burnout Buster No One Talks About

Reflection: Boundaries

Take a few minutes to think about your current relationship with boundaries:

- What comes to mind when you hear the word *boundaries*?

  ____
  ____
  ____

- Do you tend to have porous, rigid, or flexible boundaries?

  ____
  ____
  ____

- In which areas of your life (e.g., work, family, relationships) do boundaries feel hardest to set?

  ____
  ____
  ____

- How does the absence of boundaries affect your energy, mood, or mental health?

  ____
  ____
  ____

- What is one small shift you can make this week to create a healthier boundary?

  ____
  ____
  ____

Challenge Activity: Ask Yourself What You Need

- What do you need right now to feel more supported in your work or home life?

___
___
___

- What would help you feel less overwhelmed, more grounded, and more like yourself?

___
___
___
___
___
___
___
___

Now ask yourself:

- Why is it hard to ask for that?

___
___
___

- What fear arises if you ask for what you need?

___
___
___

- Now, what would you stand to gain if you asked for what you want?

___
___
___

I want you to start by asking someone you are close to for a small thing that would help you right now (E.g., Asking your mom to pick up the kids after school). Write down who you will ask and what you need. In CBT, this is called a **behavioral experiment.**

- What is the specific experiment you will try along the lines of asking someone you feel comfortable with to help you with your tasks?

  ____
  ____
  ____

- On a scale of 1–10, how uncomfortable do you feel when thinking about asking someone for support? ____________

- What do you fear will happen by asking them to help you?

  ____
  ____
  ____

- What is a possible alternative outcome?

  ____
  ____
  ____

- Now take that chance and ask the person. Write their response below:

  ____
  ____
  ____

- How uncomfortable did you feel (on a scale of 1-10) when you asked them?

  ____
  ____
  ____

- What was the outcome? Was it a response that you expected?

____

____

____

- What did you learn about yourself by doing this exercise?

____

____

____

Reflection: Honoring Your Time

Let's take a moment to reflect on your current patterns. Write down your response to these questions:

- What time-related boundary can you set to reclaim energy? (E.g., No emails after 8:00 p.m., phone off from 9:00 p.m. to 7:00 a.m., no work on Sundays.)

____

____

____

- Why would this boundary be helpful to your well-being?

____

____

____

- What would you gain by setting this boundary?

____

____

____

Challenge Activity: Reclaim Your Time

Let's make this practical. Choose *one* area this week where you'll set a new boundary:

- Shut off work notifications at ___ p.m.
- Take a real, screen-free lunch break.
- Unplug from social media one hour before bed.
- Other:_______________________________

Make a commitment to yourself. Then, each day that you set a boundary in the week, reflect on the following:

- How did you feel afterward?

  ____

- Was it uncomfortable or liberating?

  ____

- Did you feel more rested or present?

  ____

Reflection: What Drains You?

Let's take some time to pause and think about which tasks drain you and whether anything can change. Consider the following steps. Take time to think through the questions and mindfully journal your responses.

Step 1: Identify Your Level of Drain

List out your common work and home tasks.

Example:

- **Work:** responding to emails, weekly reporting, daily meetings
- **Home:** grocery shopping, bedtime routines, cooking

- Work tasks:

  ____

- Home Tasks

  ____

Then rate each one, from 0 to 100 percent, based on how much you dread doing it.

Here is a range to help you assign your level of drain:

0% Drain (Fully Energized)

- I feel completely refreshed and focused.

25% Drain (Lightly Tiring)

- I notice some effort, but it's manageable.

50% Drain (Moderately Draining)

- This task feels like work. I notice a dip in energy or motivation while doing it.

75% Drain (Highly Draining)

- I feel mentally, emotionally, or physically taxed while doing this task.

100% Drain (Completely Depleting)

- This task leaves me exhausted, overwhelmed, or burned-out.

Example:

Task: Attending a Child's School Event

- **0% Drain:** "I look forward to going, enjoy being there, and leave feeling connected."
- **25% Drain:** "It's nice, but I'm tired afterward and need a little downtime."
- **50% Drain:** "I go because I 'should,' but I feel mentally checked out and drained afterward."

- **75% Drain:** "I dread going and feel resentful about having to be there. I come home exhausted."
- **100% Drain:** "I skip the event, or go but feel numb, tearful, or completely wiped out for the rest of the day."

Now try this exercise. Assign a drain level to both your work and home tasks.

Work Tasks

Task	Drain (%)
	______%
	______%
	______%
	______%

Home Tasks

Task	Drain (%)
	______%
	______%
	______%
	______%

Now take a look. Which tasks score 70 percent or higher?

____

____

____

These likely have the biggest impact on your burnout.

Step 2: Reflect on the Impact

How do these tasks affect your energy and mood?

____

____

____

How do they spill into other parts of your life, like your sleep, relationships, or mental focus?

____

____

____

Can any of these tasks be delegated, outsourced, or restructured?

____

____

____

If you're feeling resistance about delegation, ask yourself:

- What do I fear will happen if I give this up?

  ____

  ____

  ____

- What might I gain by letting it go?

  ____

  ____

  ____

If delegation is possible:

- Is there a coworker, manager, or team member you can speak to about shifting tasks?

  ____

  ____

  ____

- Is there a family member or friend who can help lighten the load at home?

____

____

____

- If it's financially feasible, could you outsource things like cleaning, grocery delivery, or errands?

____

____

____

If delegation is not an option:

- Can you change when you do the task? (Try scheduling harder tasks for when you have the most energy.)

____

____

____

- Can you bundle it with something enjoyable? (E.g., Fold laundry while watching your favorite show.)

____

____

____

- Can you build in a small reward afterward, like a coffee or a short walk?

____

____

____

- What's one way you can make an energy-draining task feel easier?

____

____

____

Step 3: Commit to the Delegation Experiment

It is time to challenge yourself and implement some task boundaries. If letting go of control feels scary (and I understand that!), we'll start small and see what happens.

Challenge Activity: Delegation Experiment

Choose one low-risk task—at work or at home—and delegate it. Then reflect on how it went.

- Task I will delegate: ______________________________
- Who will I ask to do it: ______________________________
- What are my fears or negative thoughts about this?

  ____

  ____

  ____

- How much do I believe these fears to be true? (0–100%)

  ____

  ____

  ____

- What's an alternative, more balanced thought?

  ____

  ____

  ____

- How much do I believe this alternative thought? (0–100%) __________

Reflection: After the Delegation

Capture your responses from this experience.

- Did your worst-case fears come true? Yes / No
- What actually happened?

____

____

____

- How did you feel? Relieved, guilty, free, worried, or a mix?

  ____

  ____

  ____

- What did you learn about letting go?

  ____

  ____

  ____

Delegation isn't just about convenience; It's about preserving your well-being. Taking care of yourself benefits you and others, because you can't fully show up for others when you're running on empty.

Reflection: Who's in Your Circle?

Think about the people you spend time with. Ask yourself these questions and journal your responses:

- What do I enjoy most about the people I surround myself with?

  ____

  ____

  ____

- What makes it hard for me to decline social invites, even when I'm exhausted? *(Examples: fear of hurting feelings, fear of being alone, feeling obligated.)*

  ____

  ____

  ____

- Who makes me feel lighter and happier after spending time with them?

    1. ______________________________
    2. ______________________________
    3. ______________________________

- Who do I feel drained by after spending time with them?

    1. ______________________________
    2. ______________________________
    3. ______________________________

- Who rains on my parade when I have good news?

    ____
    ____
    ____

- Who holds space and celebrates my wins with me?

    ____
    ____
    ____

Now imagine that a close friend came to you feeling burned-out and anxious, saying they didn't have the energy to spend time with someone but felt obligated to do so.

As a loving friend, what would you tell them?

Now give that same advice to yourself.

____
____
____

Dig Deeper: Where Do Boundaries Feel Most Challenging?

As you reflect on the people in your life, take it one step further:

- In what situations do you struggle most to set boundaries?

  ____

  ____

  ____

- Are there particular people, roles, or dynamics that make it harder?

  ____

  ____

  ____

- What emotional or situational triggers lead you to overextending yourself?

  ____

  ____

  ____

Recognizing your personal boundary "blind spots" can help you plan ahead and respond more intentionally when those moments arise.

Challenge Activity: The Seven-Day Energy Audit

This week, practice using the delay tactic before saying yes to any new commitment.

Each day, reflect:

- Who did I use "Let me get back to you" with?
- How did it feel to pause before responding?
- Did I explain my boundary using self-disclosure? How did others respond?
- What did I notice about my own energy and decision-making?
- Would I use this approach again? Why or why not?

Challenge Activity: Reframe Your Statement

Think about one need and one boundary you want to communicate using the tools you just learned.

Original Statement:

(Write what you might typically say.)

____

____

____

New boundary statement with tools:

(Reframe with clarity, compassion, an "I feel" statement, and your "why" to your boundary.)

____

____

____

- What part is flexible?

  ____

- What part is non-negotiable?

  ____

- What's your deeper why?

  ____

Chapter 8: Redefining Self-Care

Reflection: What Recharges You

Capture some of your ideas of what recharges you.

Has your definition of self-care changed after reading this? If so, write down how your perspective has shifted.

Challenge Activity: Self-Care

I want you to pick any kind of self-care activity—you can make it as big or small as you want it to be. This could be something simple like sitting in the sun with tea, texting a friend you miss, or going on a short walk. Remember, this is not about numbing or taking yourself out of your current life. It is actually plugging you into the here and now—your present moment!

Write down your chosen activity:

____

Now follow these steps:

1. Schedule time for your selected activity (I recommend inserting it on your calendar.)
2. You also can share your scheduled time here: _____________
3. When the time comes, don't cancel it. Set a timer for 5 minutes.
4. Do the activity. Fully engaging, without multitasking.
5. Then complete the Reflection: Post Self-Care Pause questions.

Reflection: Post Self-Care Pause

- How did you feel afterward? Energized? Calm? Centered?

____

____

____

- Did any unexpected emotions surface?

____

____

____

- What would it mean for you to continue prioritizing this activity?

____

____

____

- How can you realistically make time for this in your daily life?

____

____

____

Reflection: Setting Your Temperature

Ask yourself:

- What would it look like if you set the tone for your day?

  ____

  ____

  ____

- What do you want to change for you to set your "temperature?"

  ____

  ____

  ____

- Describe your ideal morning ritual. What does "setting your temperature" look like?

  ____

  ____

  ____

Chapter 9: Self-Compassion

Reflection: Applying Self-Compassion

Dr. Kristin Neff, a pioneering researcher and scholar in self-compassion defines self-compassion with three core elements:

- Self-Kindness vs. Self-Judgment
- Common Humanity vs. Isolation
- Mindfulness vs. Over-Identification

Consider Dr. Neff's three-part definition:

- Have you used self-compassion before? What was it like? If you can't think of a time, what do you imagine it would feel like to practice it?

___

___

___

- Which of the three elements—self-kindness, common humanity, or mindfulness—feels hardest for you to practice? Why?

___

___

___

- Recall a recent moment of stress, failure, or burnout. How different would you have felt if you had responded to yourself with compassion rather than criticism?

___

___

___

Challenge Activity: Write Your Self-Compassion Letter

Prompts for Your Self-Compassion Letter

- What do you want to thank yourself for? Acknowledge the strength and resilience that have brought you to where you are today.
- What feelings are you experiencing right now? Normalize them as part of the human experience.
- What obstacles have you overcome in your life? Give yourself credit for your perseverance.
- What do you need to forgive yourself for? What are you ready to release?
- How can you express gratitude for your body and all it has done for you?
- What have you learned from your triumphs and struggles?
- Moving forward, how can you be kinder to yourself in this next chapter of your life?

My Self-Compassion Letter

Reflection: The Self-Compassion Letter

After completing your letter, take a moment to pause and reflect on the experience.

- How did you feel after writing your letter? Better, worse, or neutral?

____
____
____
____
____
____
____

- What were some key takeaways you received from writing this letter?

____
____
____
____
____
____

- Does this tool resonate for you in your burnout journey? Why or why not?

____
____
____
____
____
____

Chapter 10: Visualizing Your Future Self

Challenge Activity: Envision Your Future Self

Now it's your turn. Find a quiet place and give yourself permission to dream without limitations, fear, or guilt about your future self. Take 10–15 minutes to reflect on these questions:

- **Six months from now:** What does my life look like? What am I doing that brings energy and joy? How is it different from today?
- **Two years from now:** What does my life look like? How do I feel? Who is beside me? What supports or inspires me? If I'm still in the same career, what has shifted to make it more fulfilling?
- **Five years from now:** What parts of my life light me up? What brings me ease, meaning, and joy?

Visualization gives us a focal point that pulls us forward and reminds us that burnout doesn't need to define our life permanently.

Reflection: Your Future Self

It's time to take the vision you've created and write it down. Capture it before it fades so you can return to it again and again as a guide.

- What do you want your future self to look like?

  ____

  ____

  ____

- What habits are you cultivating now that will lead you there?

  ____

  ____

  ____

- What new habits do you need to develop?

  ____

  ____

  ____

Chapter 11: Living in Alignment with Your Values

Reflection: Core Values

Now take a moment to reflect on the values you selected.

- What did you learn about yourself when you identified these values?

____
____
____
____

- How do you currently express these values in your life?

____
____
____
____

- In what ways does your work align—or not align—with these values?

____
____
____
____

- Are there habits, relationships, or routines that conflict with what matters most to you?

____
____
____
____

- Are there values you deeply care about but haven't prioritized?

____
____
____
____

Challenge Activity: Align with Your Values

It is time to bring more alignment into your life with your values. This activity will help you put together a plan to do this.

1. **Choose your top five values.**

    1. ______________________________
    2. ______________________________
    3. ______________________________
    4. ______________________________
    5. ______________________________

2. **Now rank them on a scale of 1 to 5**

    (1 = Not living it at all, 5 = Fully aligned).

Values	Rank

3. **For these values, ask yourself these questions:**

- What small steps can I take to integrate this value more into my daily life?

    ____

    ____

    ____

    ____

- What obstacles prevent me from living this value fully?

  ____
  ____
  ____
  ____

- How can I restructure my priorities to honor what matters most?

  ____
  ____
  ____
  ____

Chapter 12: Honoring Change and Adaptation in the Seasons of Our Lives

Reflection: Your Life Season

Take a few quiet moments to reflect on where you are, and how you can adapt with care. Consider these questions and write down your responses.

- Is there a value you're currently pushing yourself to uphold, even though it's draining you?

  ____
  ____
  ____

- What would it look like to honor that value in a different way during your current season of life?

  ____
  ____
  ____

- What do you need to accept about this current season of your life in order to move through this phase with more ease?

____
____
____

- How might softening your approach to living your values bring you more peace and fulfillment?

____
____
____

Challenge Activity: Seasons of Your Life

Now that you've reflected on your current season, let's explore how to bring your values into this chapter of life.

- **Name Your Season:** What would you call this chapter of your life right now? (E.g., healing, transition, rebuilding, quiet joy.)

____
____
____

- **Describe it in Three Words:** Honest words that capture your reality. (E.g., foggy, slow, sacred.)

____
____
____

- **Create a Mantra or Phrase:** Something simple that feels like a hand on your heart. (E.g., "I'm allowed to rest;" "Gentle is still strong;" "I don't have to rush.")

____
____
____

- **Choose One Small Act:** A walk, a phone call, canceling something, setting a timer for rest, or whatever feels supportive right now.

____
____
____

Chapter 13: The Power of Small Wins

Reflection: Noticing Your Small Wins

Now that we know the powerful research about filtering and focusing on the small wins, let's take a moment to reflect on building our small-wins muscle.

To help you reflect on your small wins, consider these questions:

1. What small win, no matter how minor, can you acknowledge from today or this week? (E.g., I got out of bed on a hard day, I responded to an email I was avoiding, I asked for help.)

   ____
   ____
   ____

2. When you think back on your week, what moments of effort, progress, or resilience did you overlook because you were focused on what went wrong?

   ____
   ____
   ____

3. What specific action can you commit to over the next seven days to build your "positive filter" muscle? (**Tip:** Start a small wins journal or simply jot one win per day on your calendar.)

   ____
   ____
   ____

4. Can you think of a small win in your past that eventually led to a bigger transformation?

____

____

____

5. How can you intentionally celebrate your small wins moving forward?

____

____

____

Challenge Activity: Celebrate the Small Wins

Now that you have an idea of how much the small-wins-lens shows up in your life, I want you to practice this skill over the next seven days. Write down one win you accomplished each day. If you need ideas, revisit the list of small wins reviewed earlier.

Monday Small Win: ______________________

Tuesday Small Win: ______________________

Wednesday Small Win: ______________________

Thursday Small Win: ______________________

Friday Small Win: ______________________

Saturday Small Win: ______________________

Sunday Small Win: ______________________

Remember, the more we focus on the good we've done, the more we create a positive filter in our brain. This awareness of the good provides momentum, moving us closer to the life we want to live.

Chapter 14: Reintegrating into Life after Burnout

Challenge Activity: Relapse Prevention Burnout Plan

This is your opportunity to become crystal clear on what matters most and what you refuse to sacrifice again.

Ask yourself:

What are your top three priorities for your well-being?

1. ______________________________

2. ______________________________

3. ______________________________

What boundaries will you set around work, relationships, and personal time?

____

____

____

What is one thing you absolutely will not compromise on again?

____

____

____

These nonnegotiables are your foundation. They are your anchors moving forward.

Reflection: Create a Sustainable Routine

You don't need a "perfect" schedule. You need a sustainable rhythm—one that includes rest, joy, movement, and meaningful work, not just busyness and productivity.

Reflect on:

- What does an ideal, balanced day look like for you?

  ____

  ____

  ____

- How can you build in rest *before* you need it?

  ____

  ____

  ____

- What small, grounding habits can anchor your day?

  ____

  ____

  ____

- Do you have agency over what your days look like?
  - What small steps can I take to integrate this value more into my daily life?

    ____

    ____

    ____

  - What obstacles prevent me from living this value fully?

    ____

    ____

    ____

Reflection: Identify Warning Signals and Personal Triggers

From these lists, or from your own awareness, list out your warning signals and personal triggers.

My warning signals are:

____

____

____

My personal triggers are:

____

____

____

Reflection: Shift Your Mindset

One of the trickiest traps during post-burnout is slipping back into the belief that your worth equals your output.

This was my Achilles' heel. But here's what I've learned: *You are valuable without constantly achieving. Your rest is your recharge time.*

Reflect on these questions:

- How will I remind myself that rest is productive and beneficial?
- How can I cultivate presence, not just performance?
- What outdated beliefs about productivity do I need to unlearn?

www.ingramcontent.com/pod-product-compliance
Ingram Content Group UK Ltd.
Pitfield, Milton Keynes, MK11 3LW, UK
UKHW061954290726
14090UKWH00021B/1223

9 798218 922665